NEGATIVE SPACE

NEGATIVE SPACE
è pubblicato in occasione della mostra *Mungo Thomson: Negative Space Variations*,
per la serie di mostre *Eldorado*, progetti inediti di giovani artisti internazionali.

NEGATIVE SPACE
is published on the occasion of the exhibition *Mungo Thomson: Negative Space Variations*,
for the exhibition series *Eldorado*, site-specific projects by international emerging artists.

GAMeC – Galleria d'Arte Moderna e Contemporanea di Bergamo
13 ottobre 2006 – 25 febbraio 2007
october 13 2006 – february 25 2007

a cura di / curated by:
ALESSANDRO RABOTTINI

con il generoso sostegno di / with the generous support of:
AMITIÉ SANS FRONTIÈRE, BERGAMO
MARGO LEAVIN GALLERY, LOS ANGELES

un ringraziamento particolare a / a special thanks to:
JOHN CONNELLY PRESENTS, NEW YORK
DAN CAMERON

Ideazione / Conception:
MUNGO THOMSON

Edito da / Edited by:
CHRISTOPH KELLER

Editore / Publisher:
JRP|RINGIER, ZÜRICH

Stampatore / Printer:
MUSUMECI S.P.A., QUART (AOSTA)

Graphic Design:
MUNGO THOMSON with PURTILL FAMILY BUSINESS

questa pubblicazione è parte della serie di libri d'artista /
this publication is part of the artists' books series
CHRISTOPH KELLER EDITIONS
published by JRP|Ringier Kunstverlag AG, Zürich

ISBN:
10: 3-905770-27-X
13: 978-3-905770-27-8

MUNGO THOMSON

NEGATIVE SPACE

CHRISTOPH KELLER EDITIONS

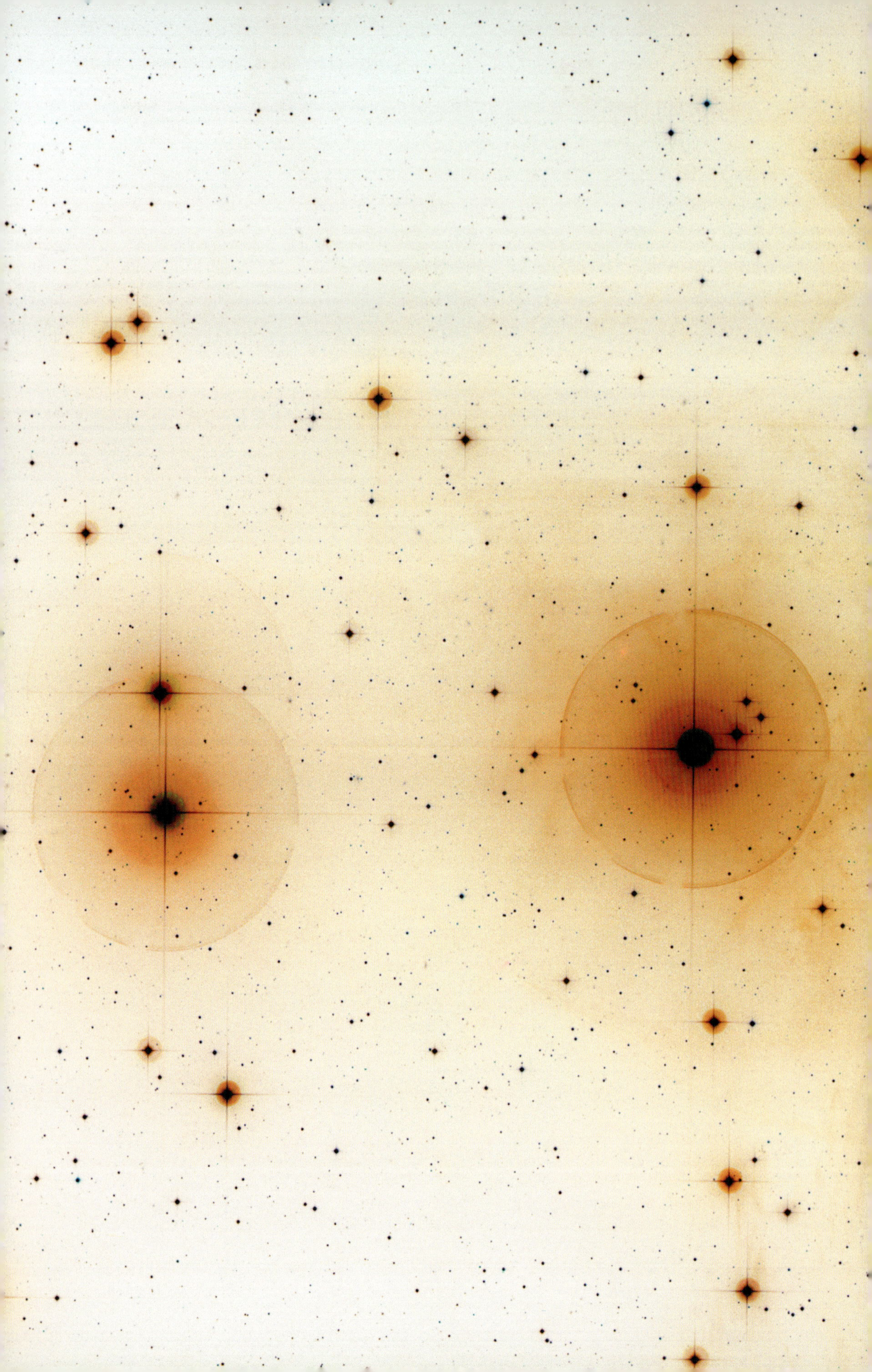

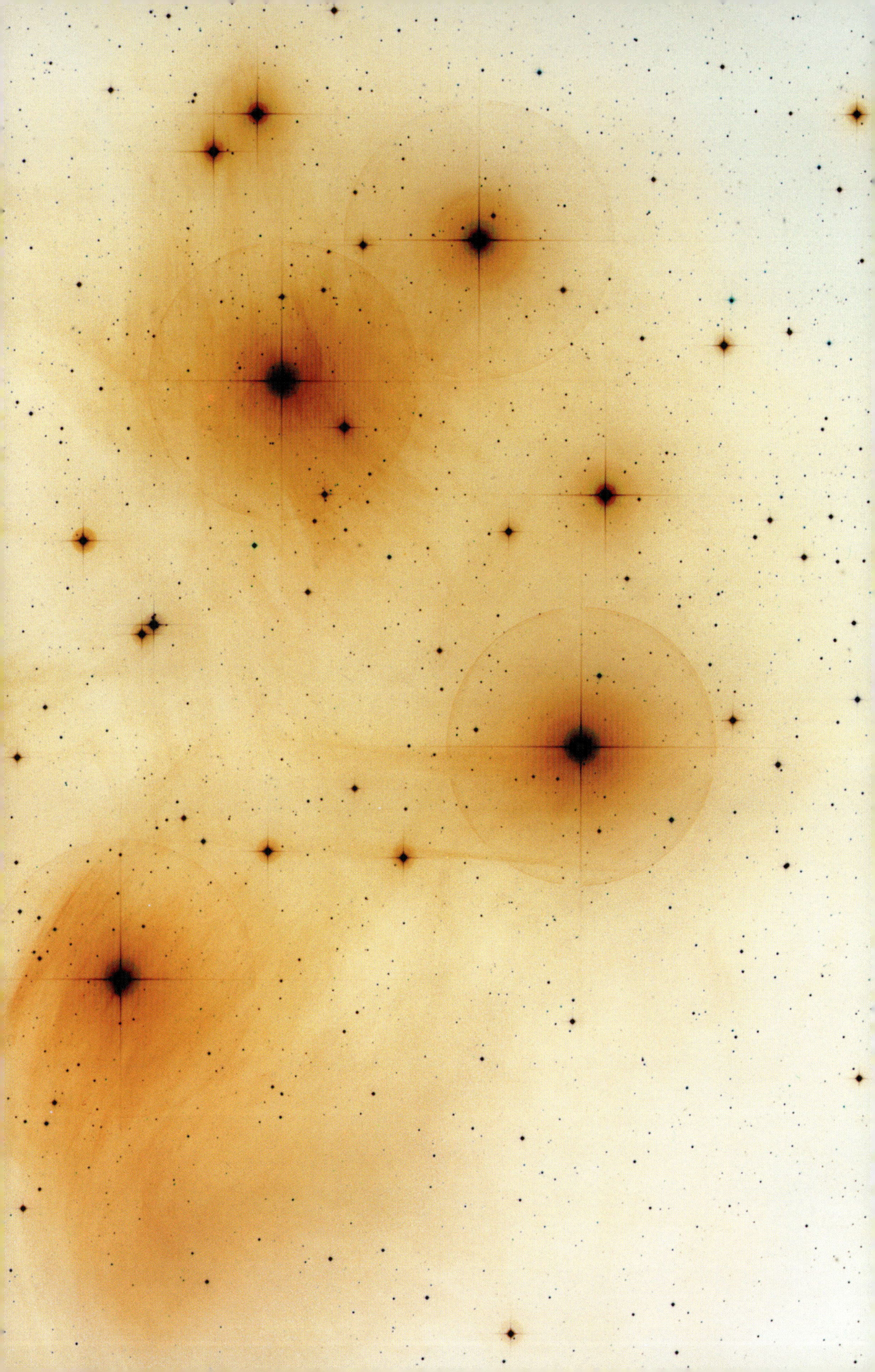

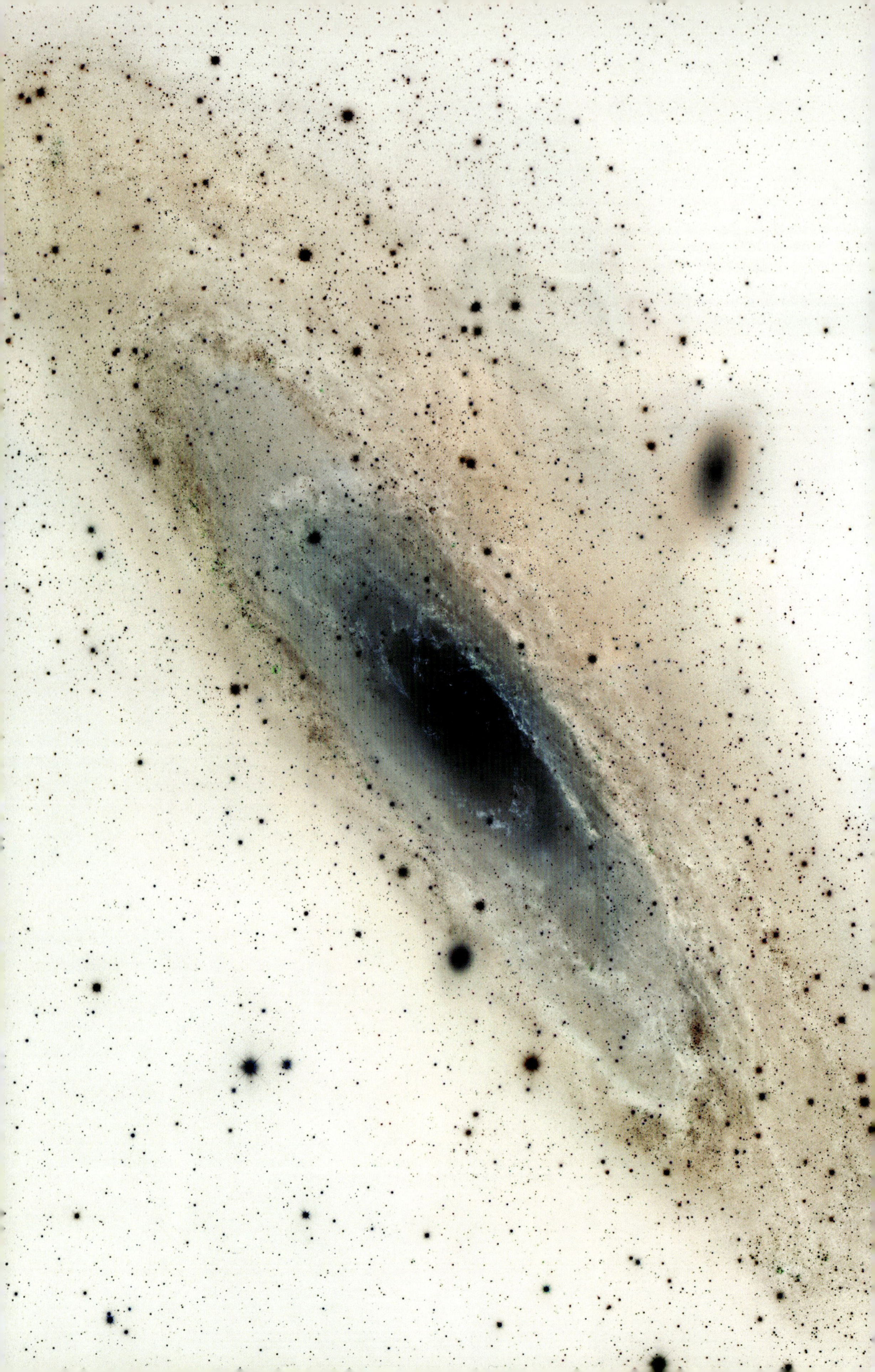

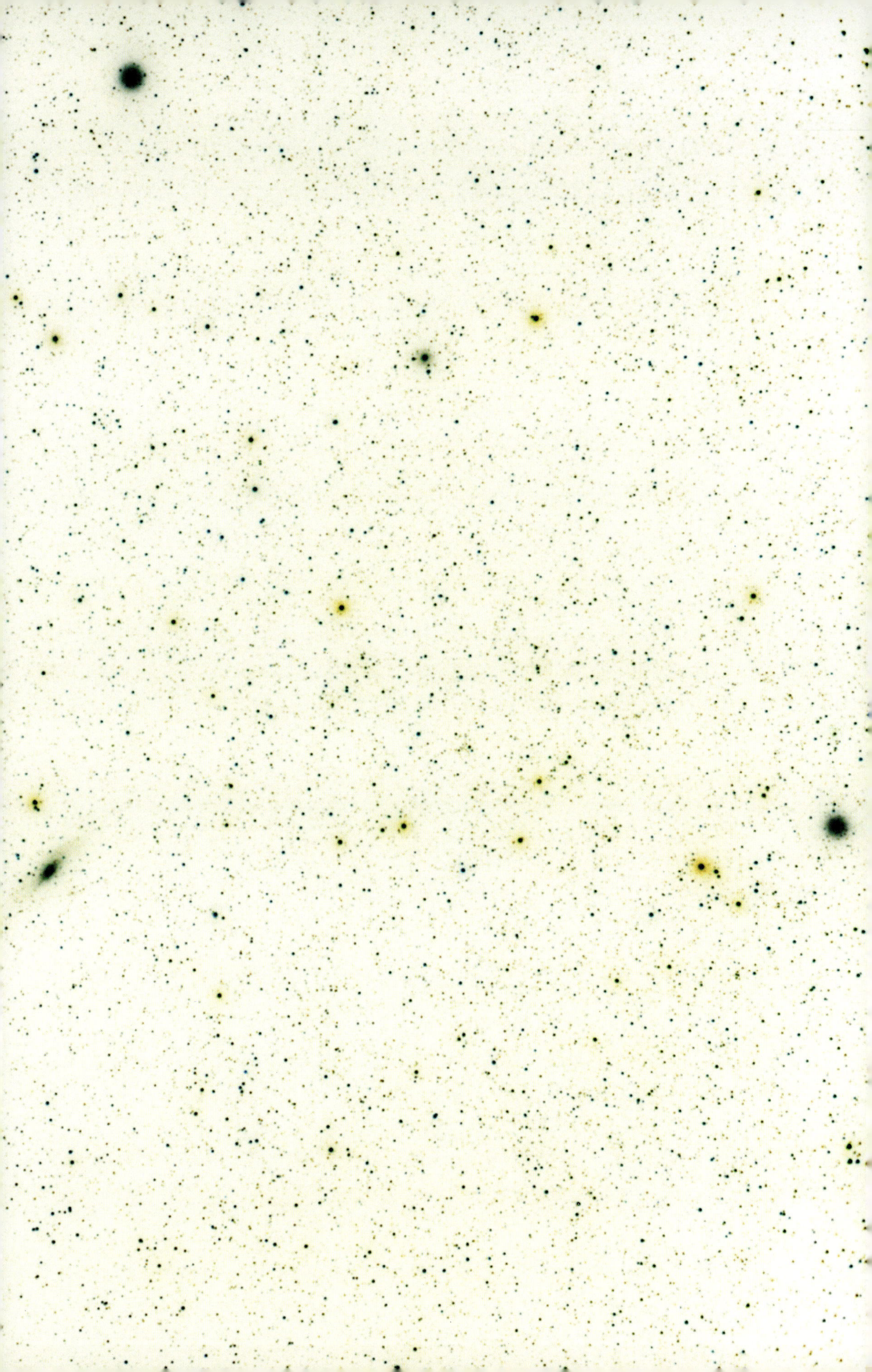

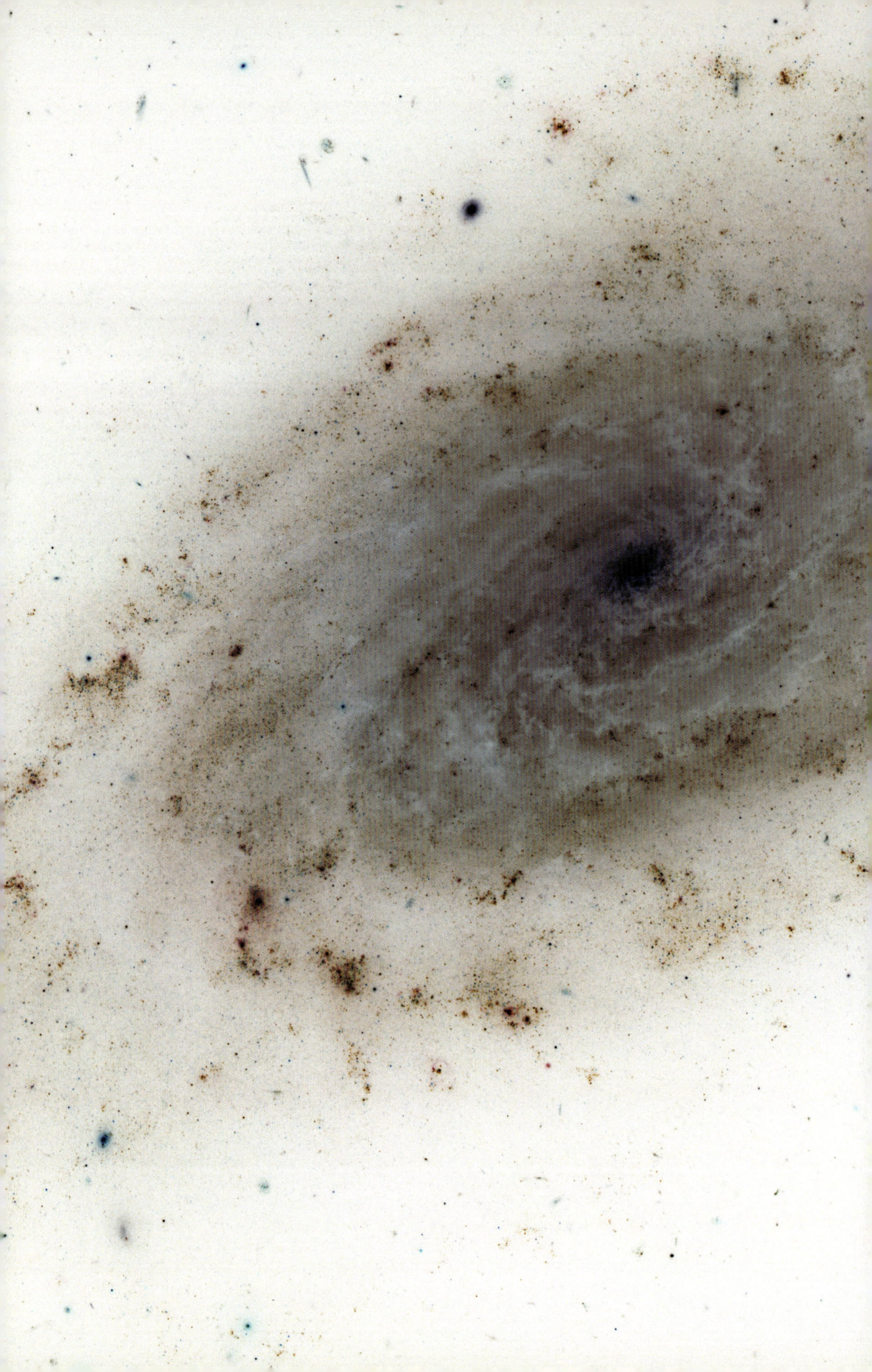

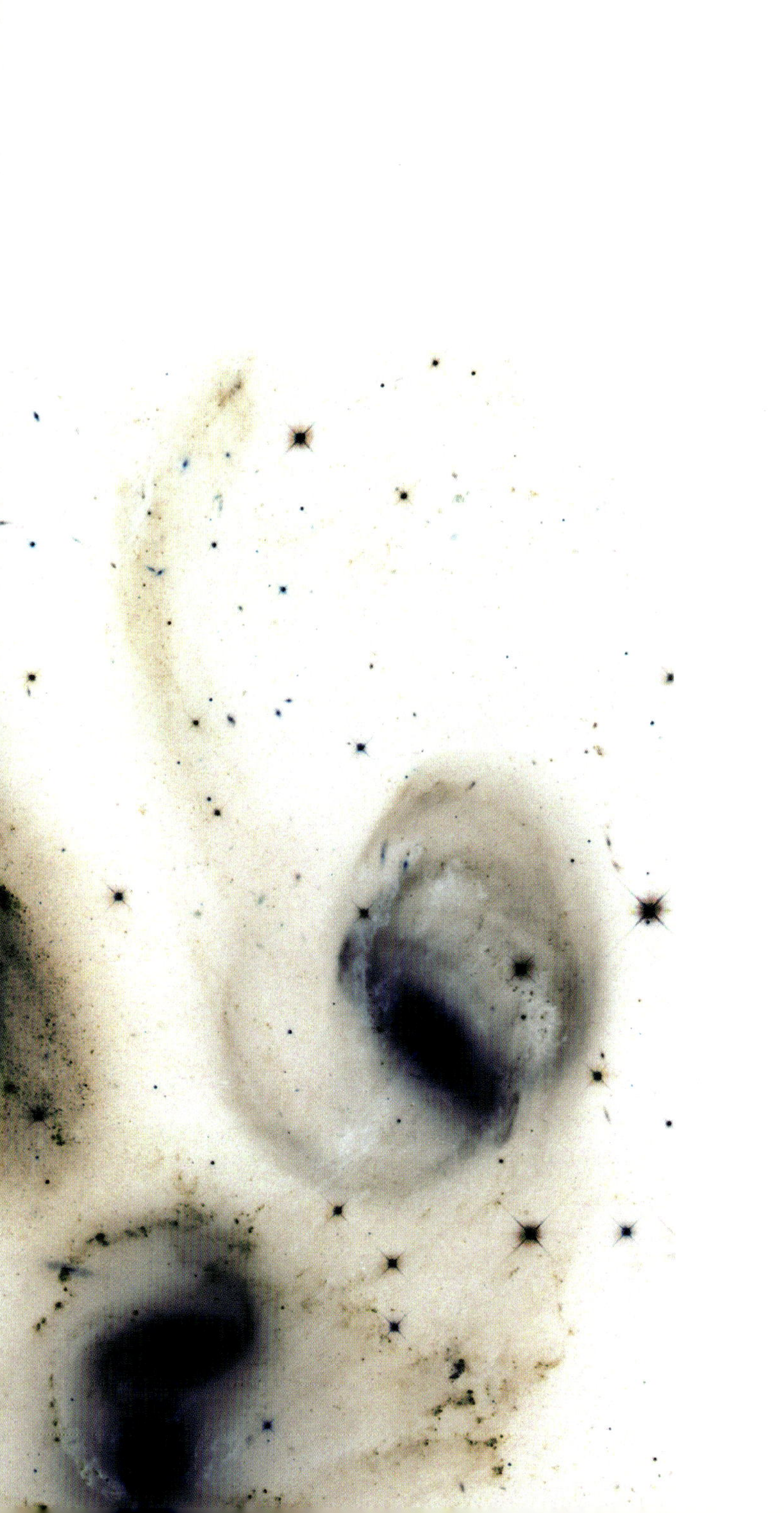

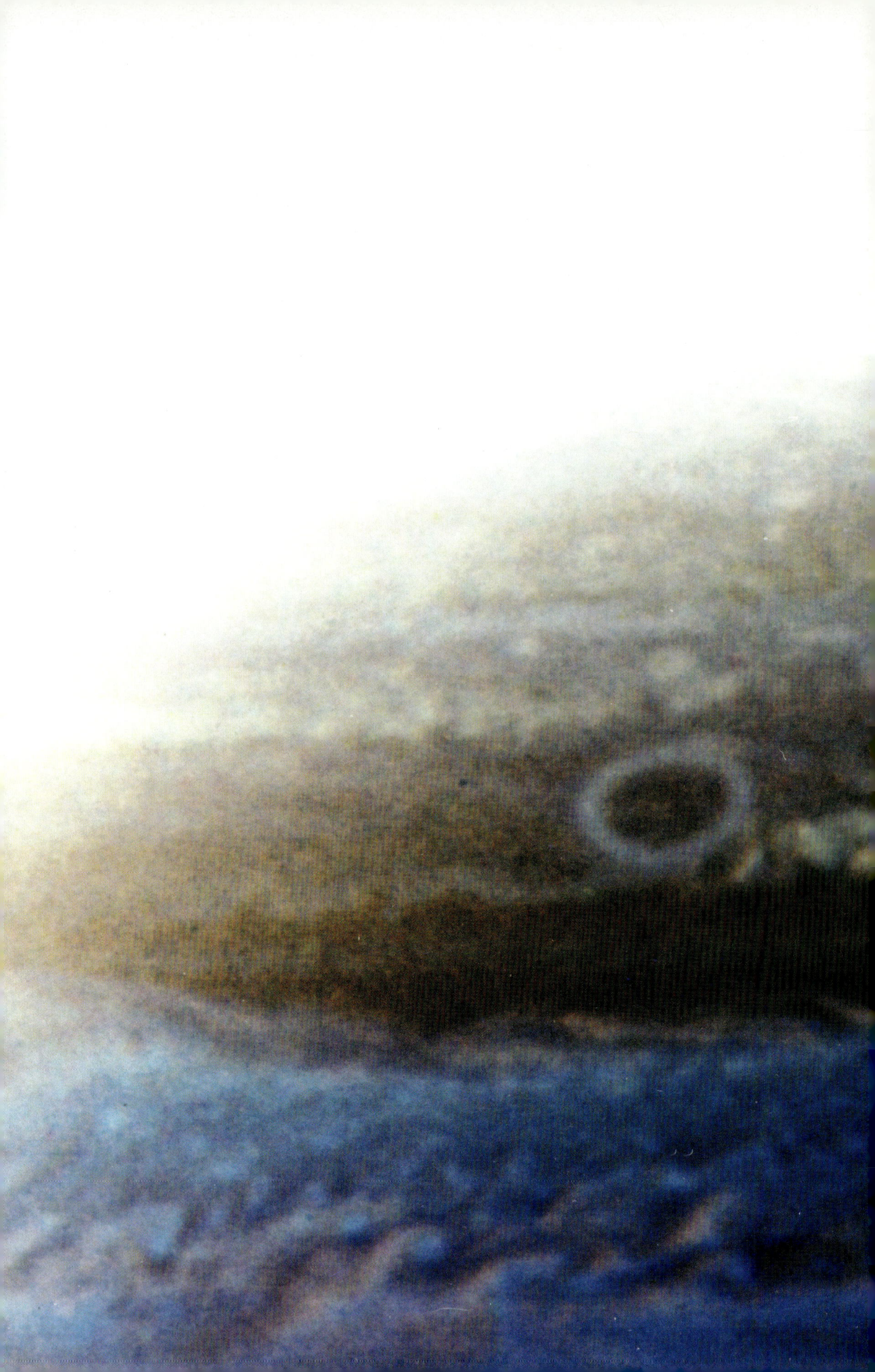

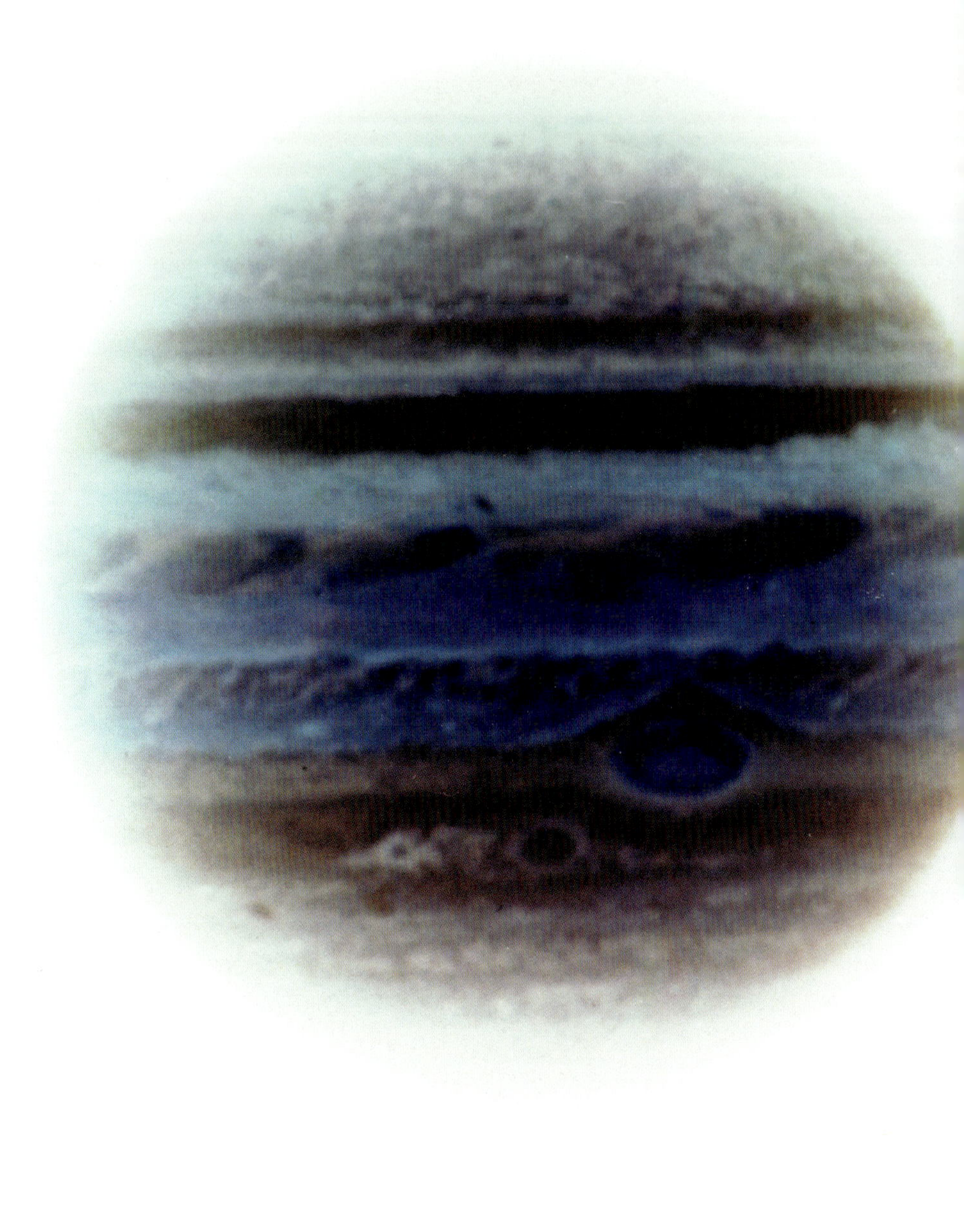

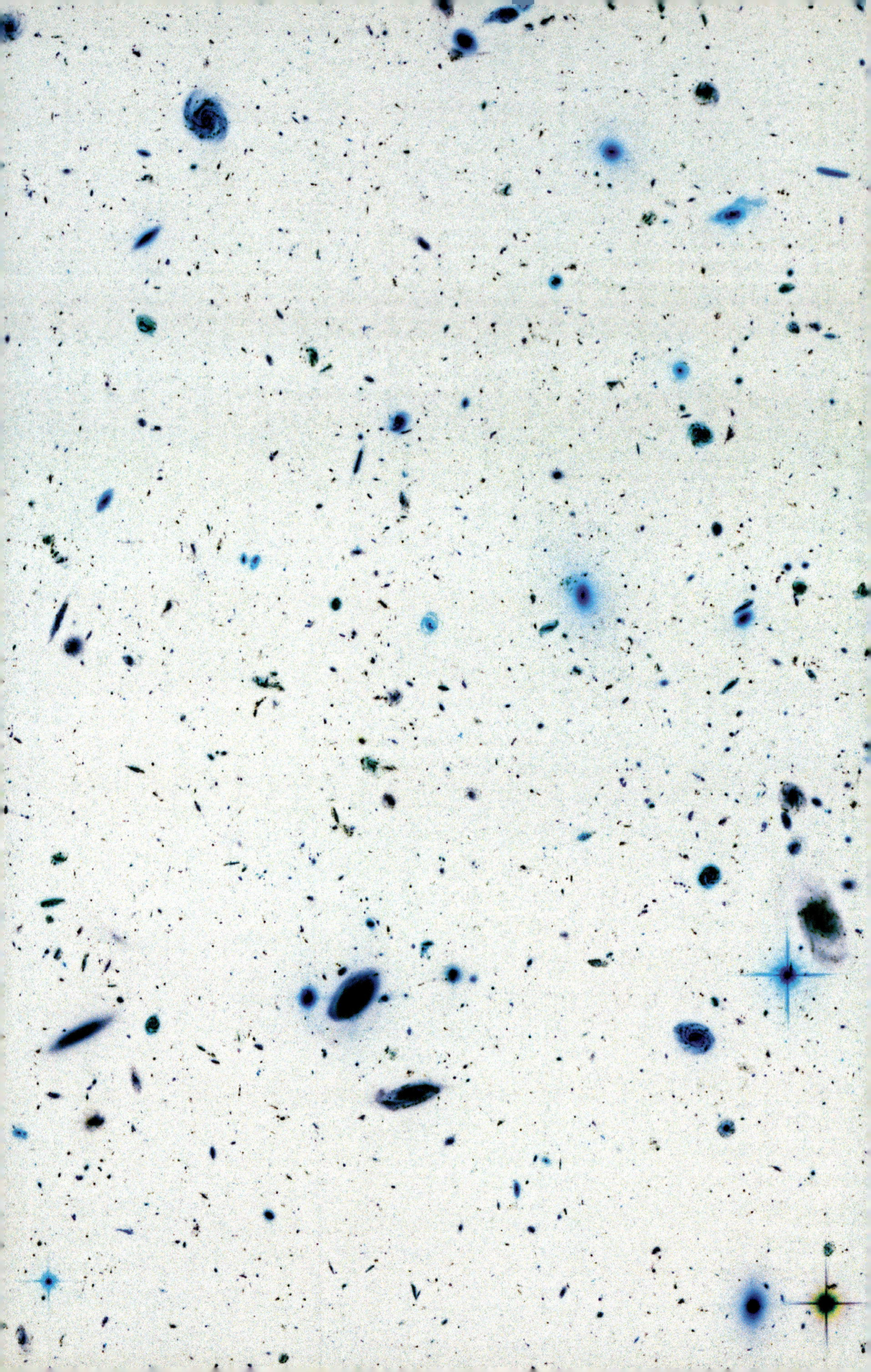

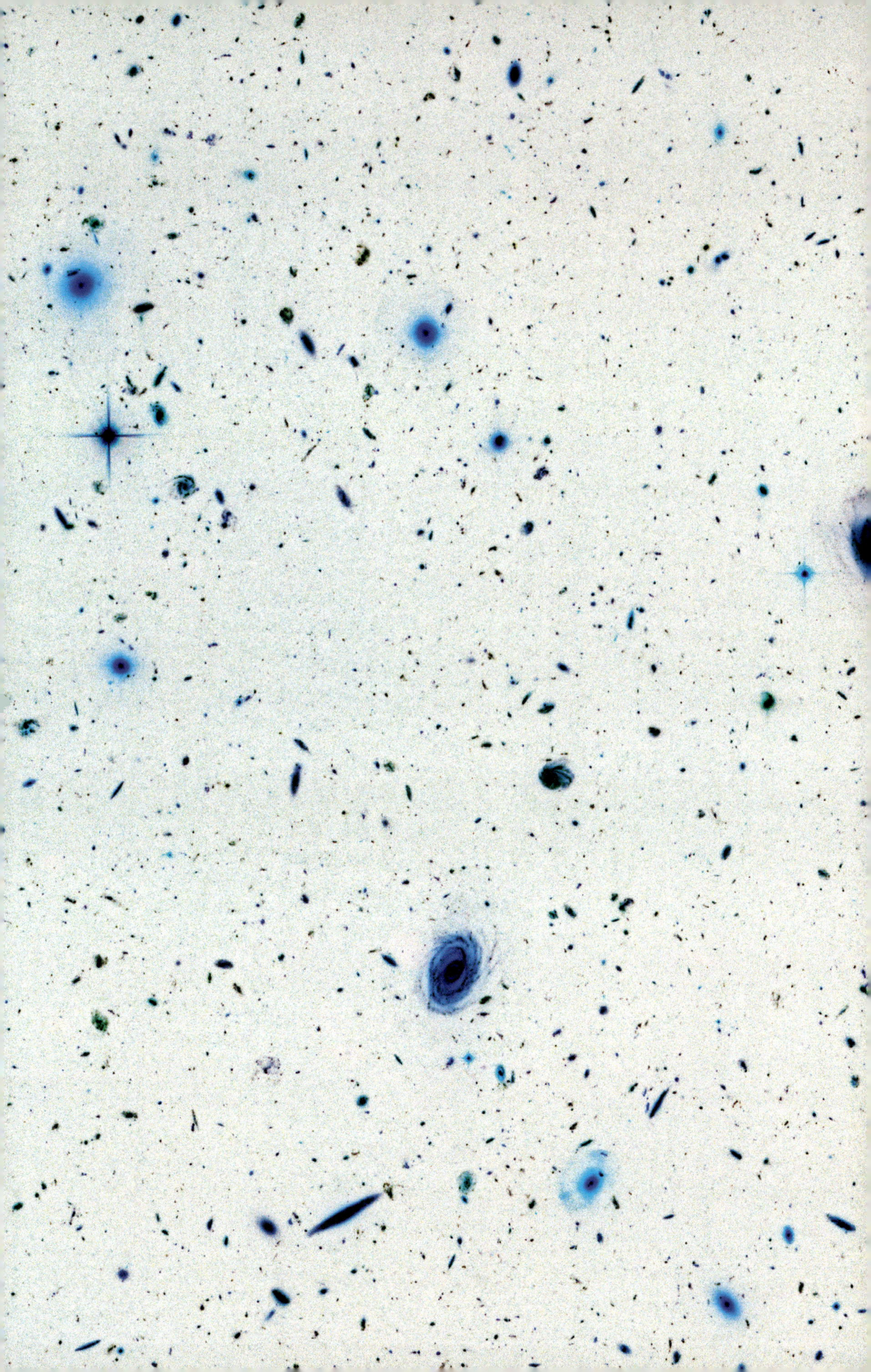

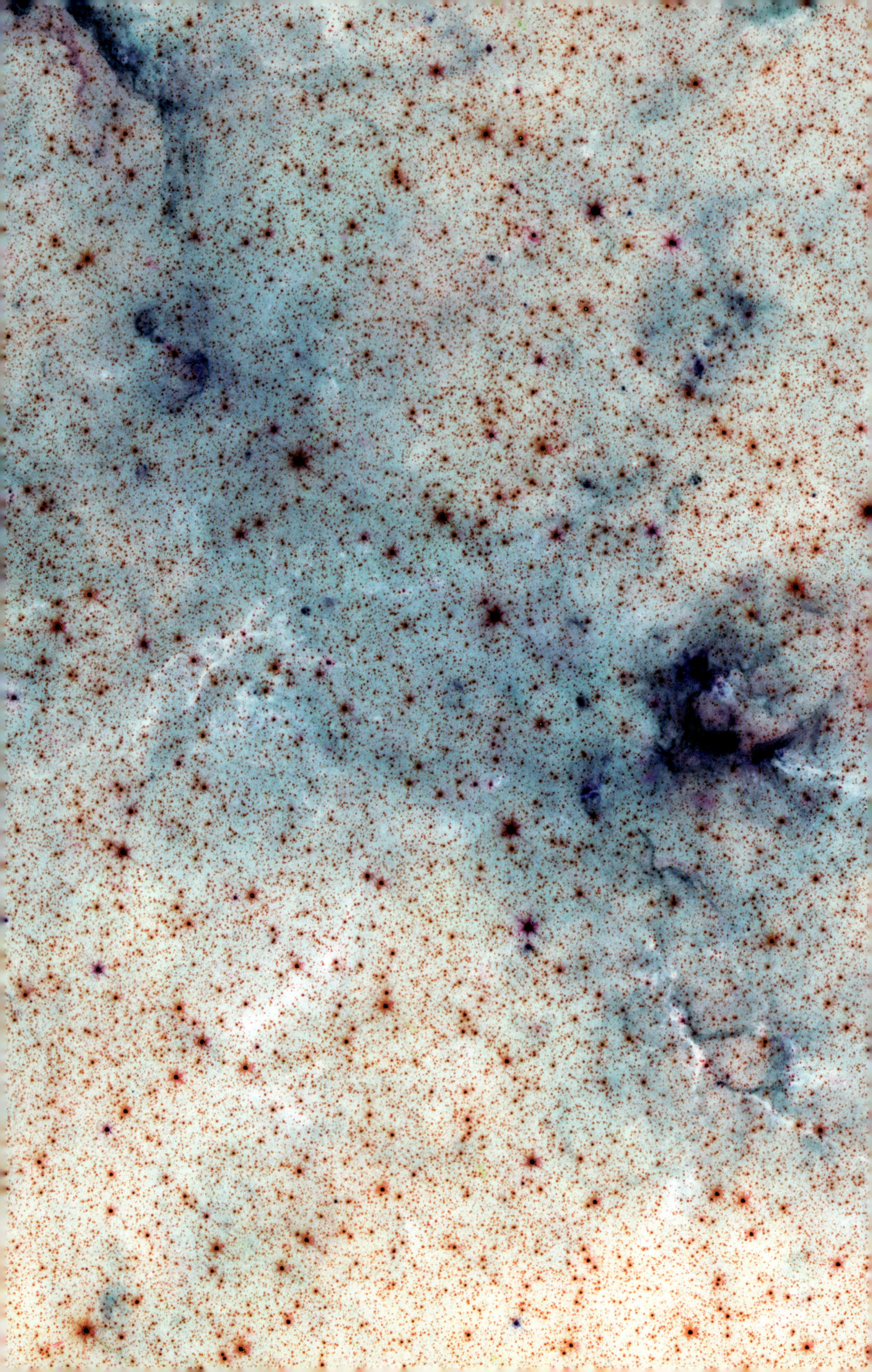

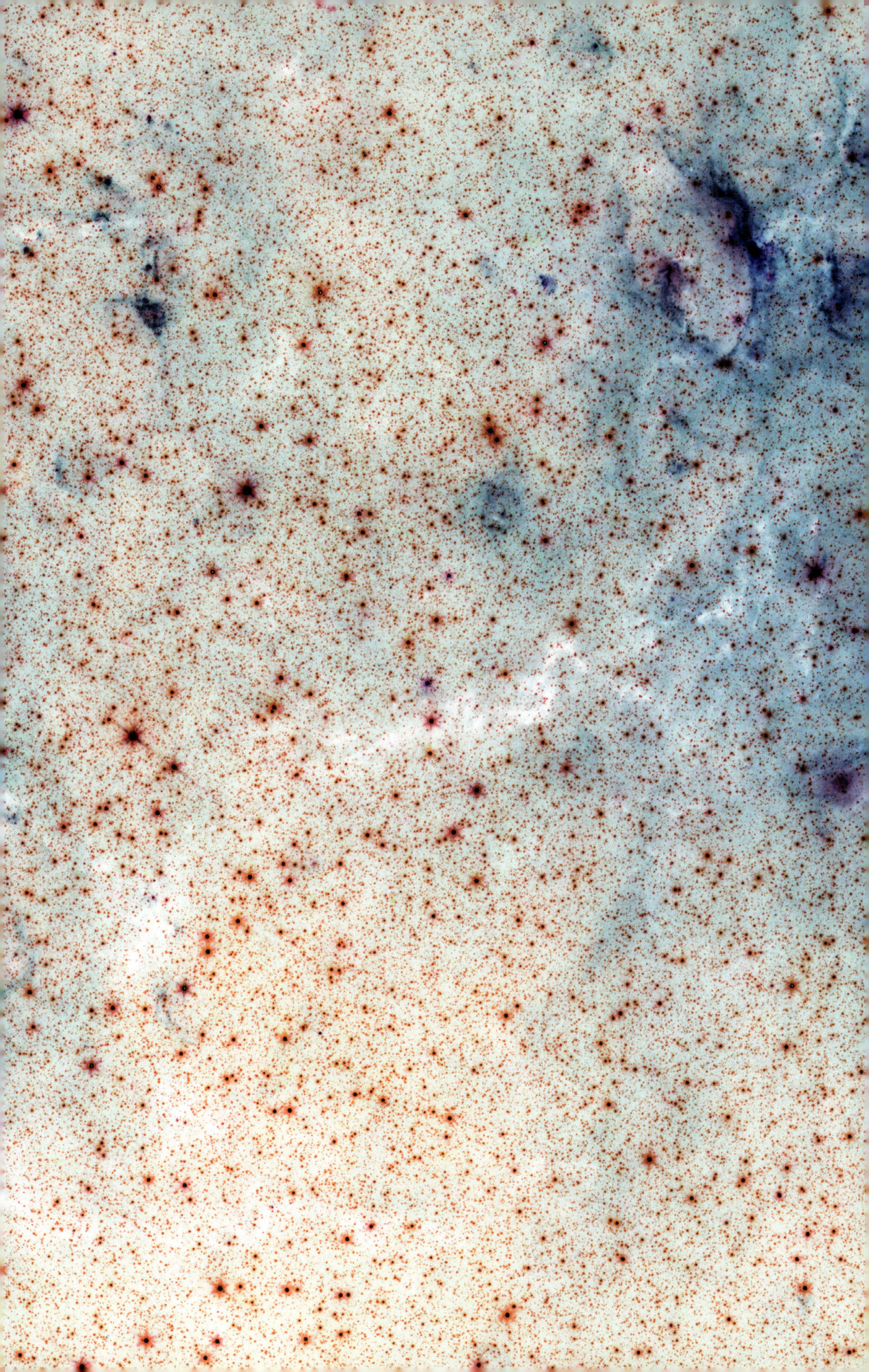

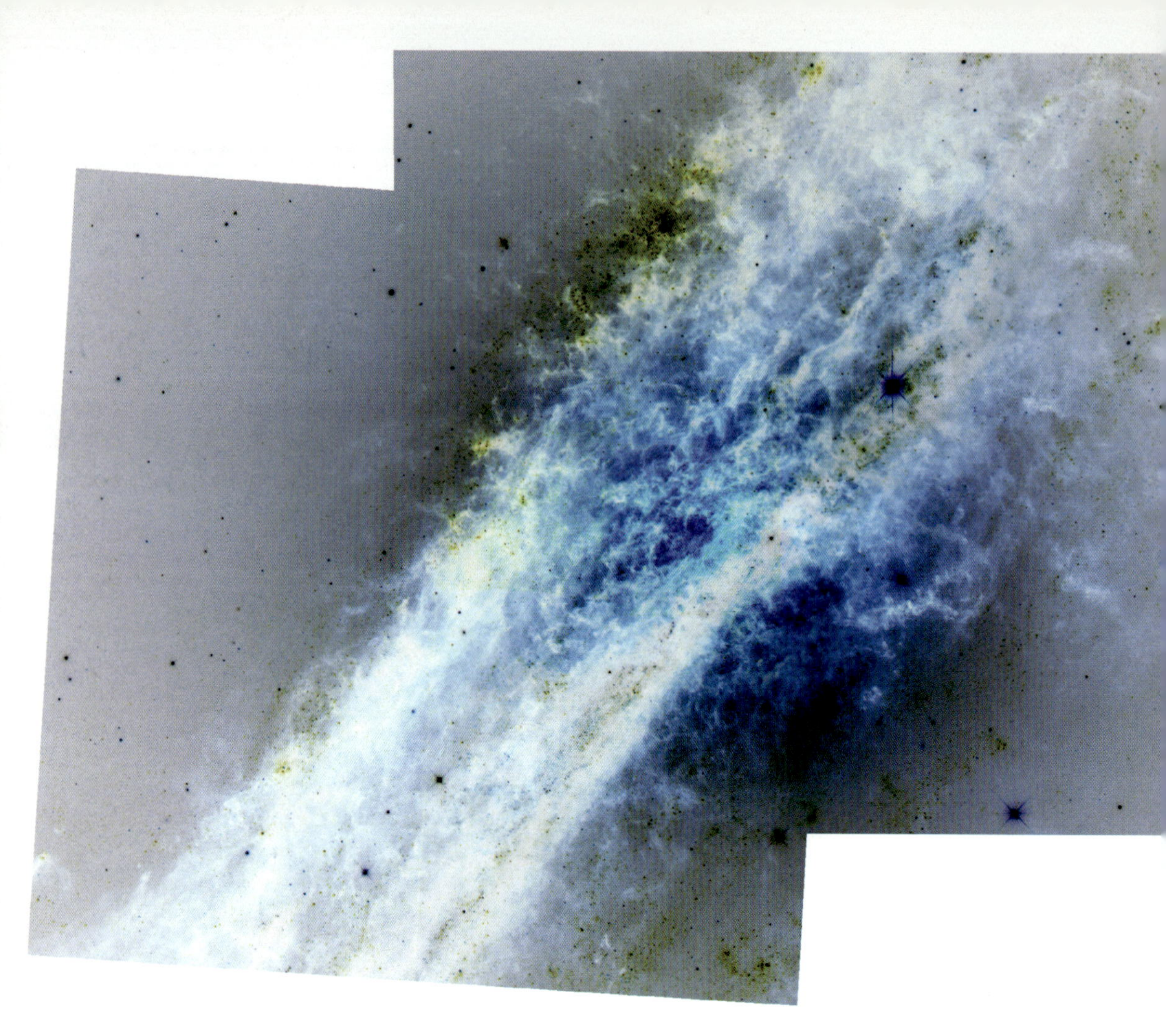

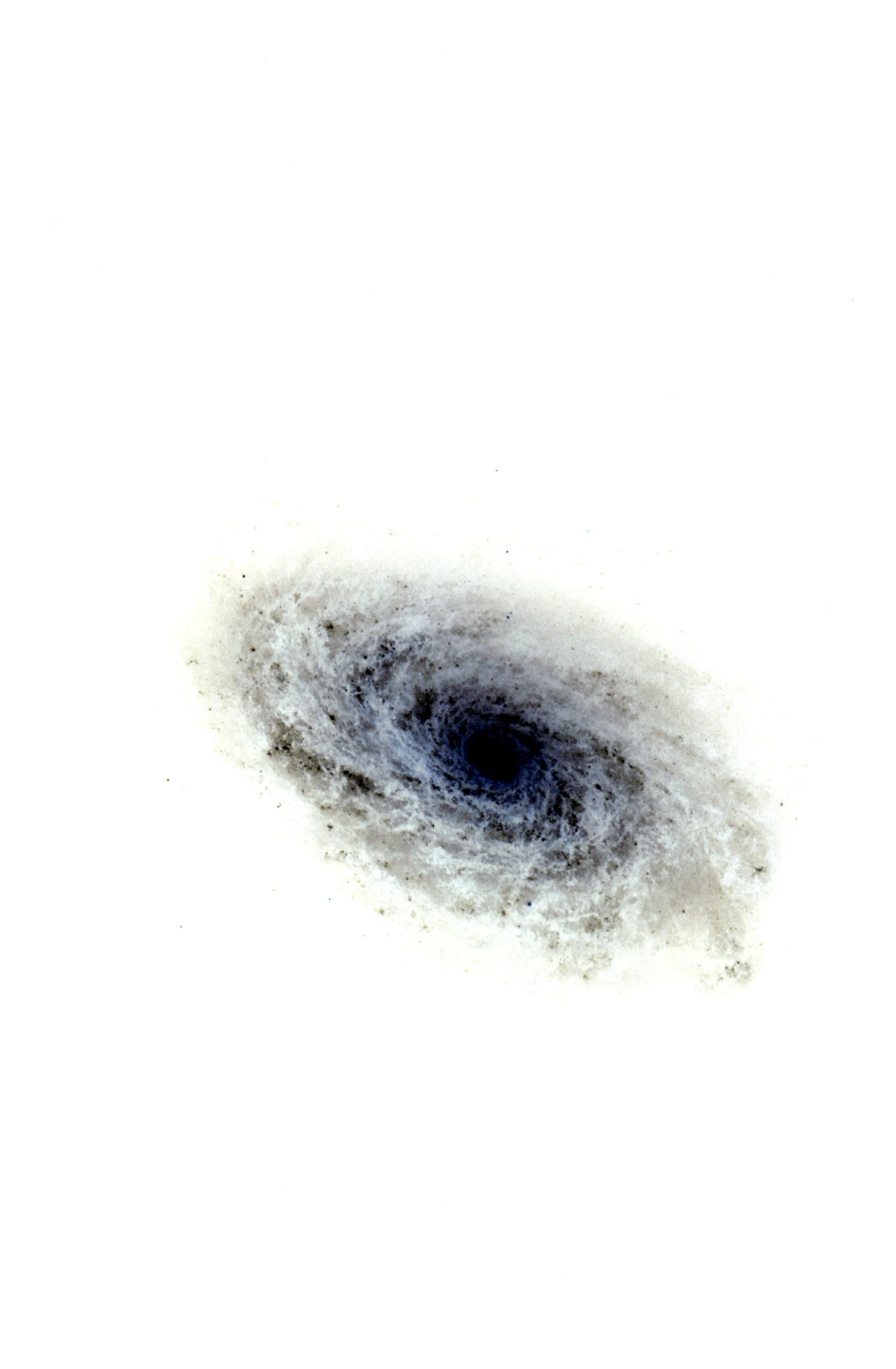

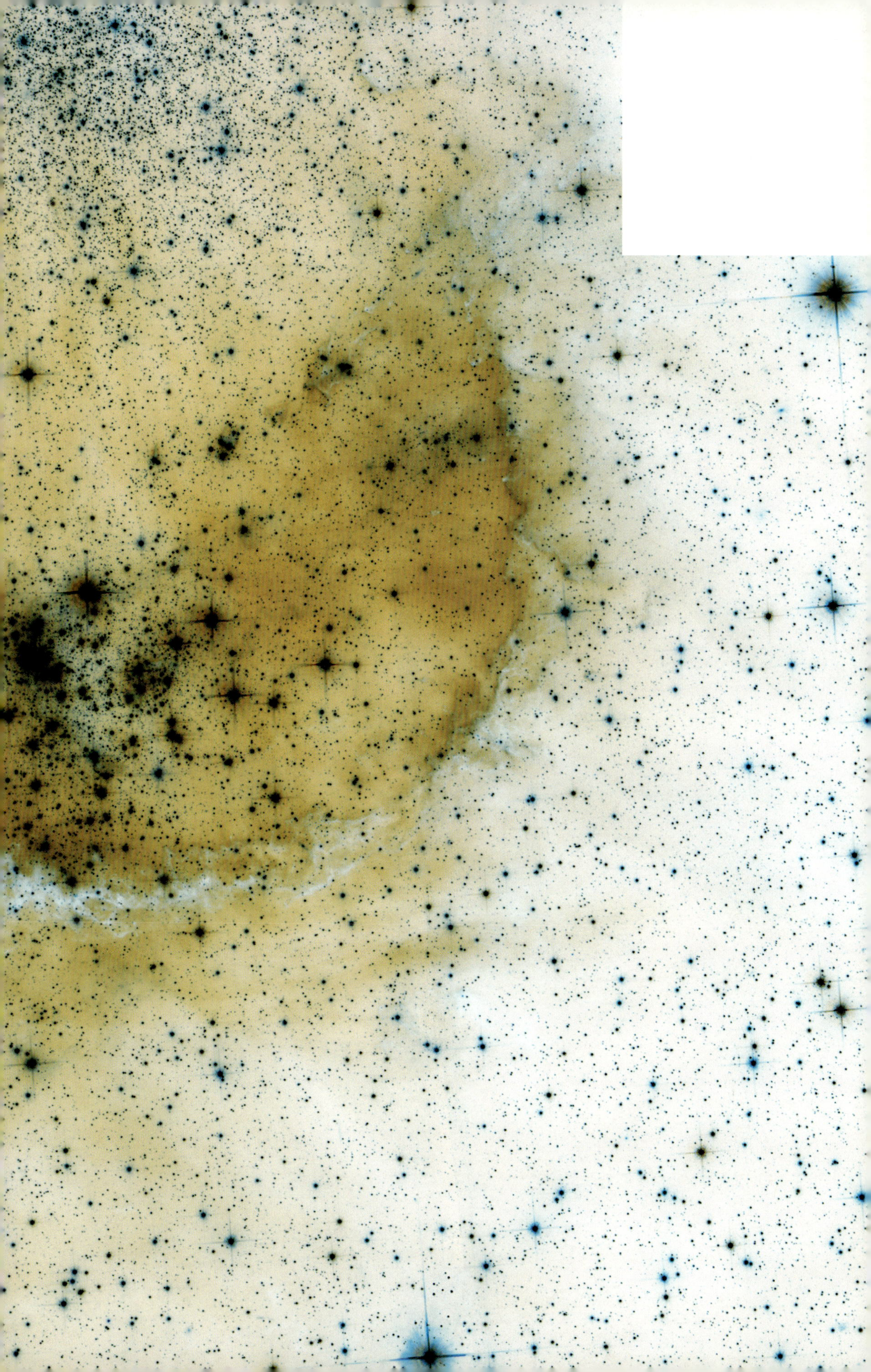

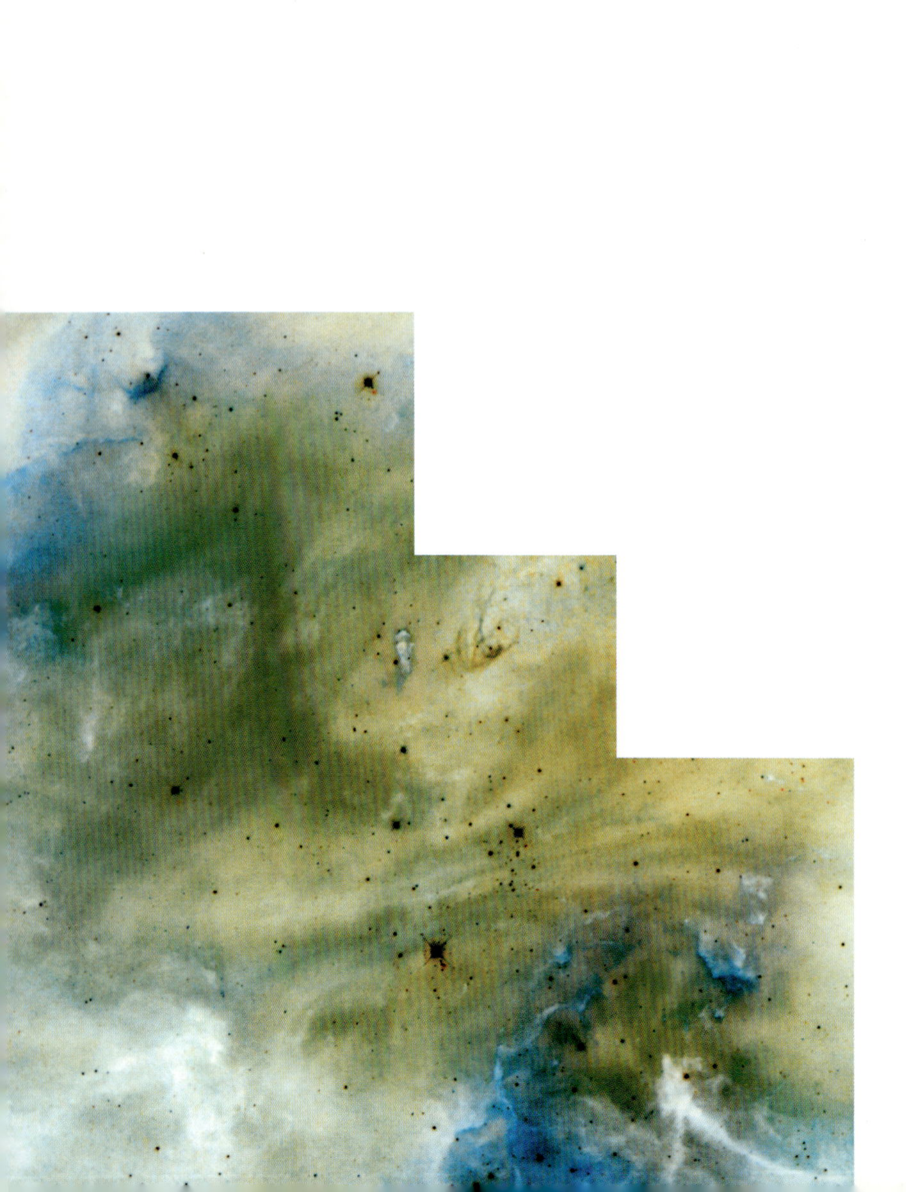

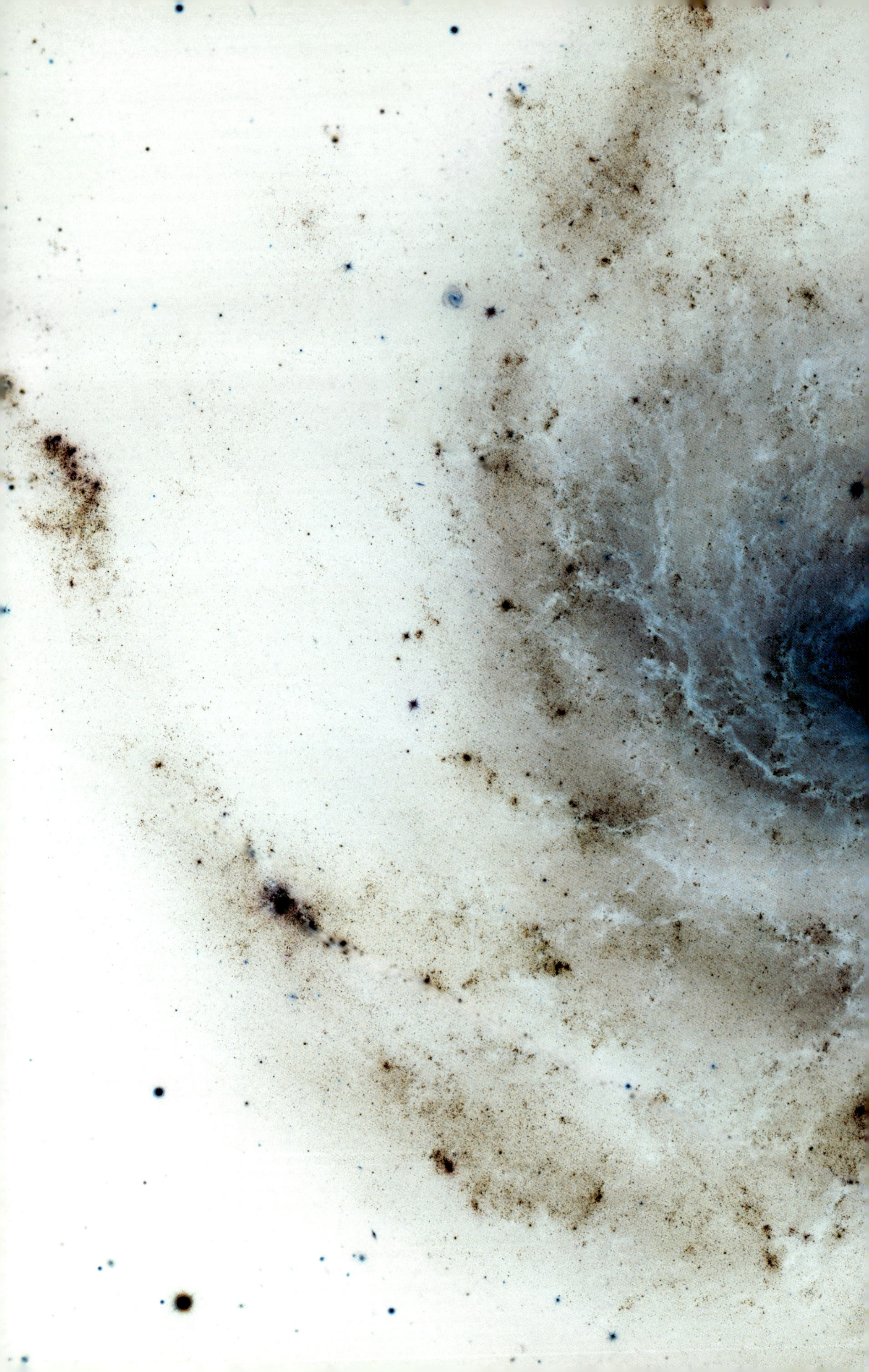

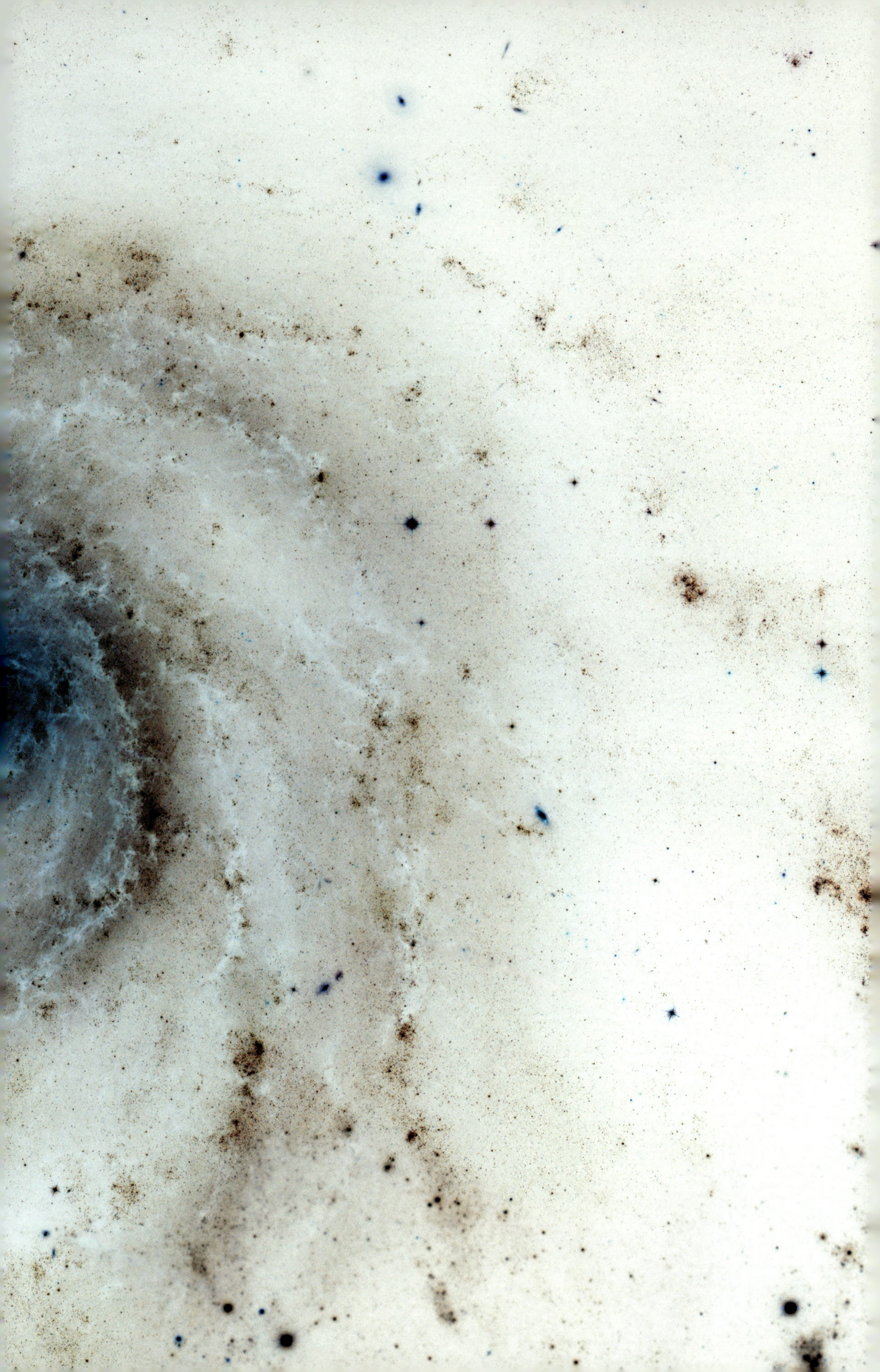

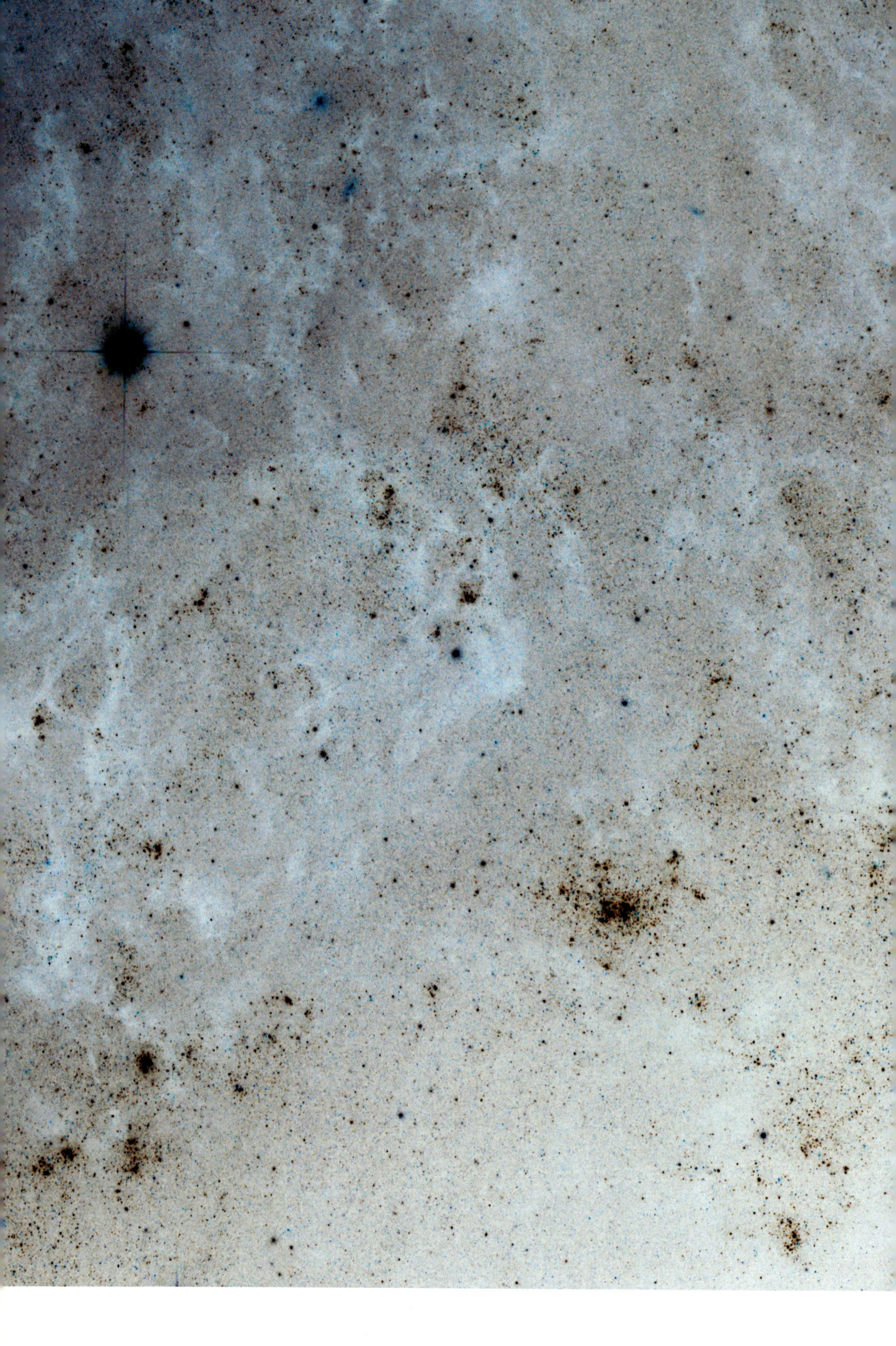

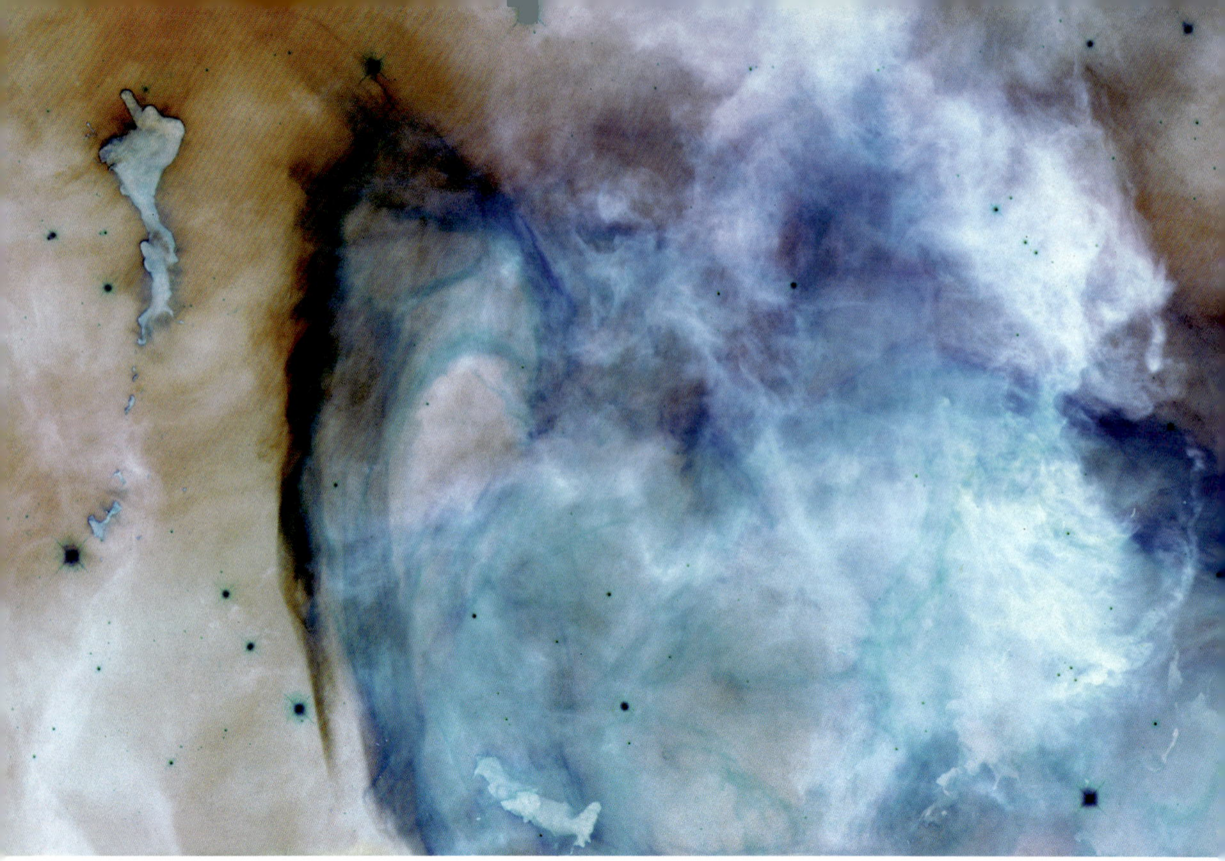

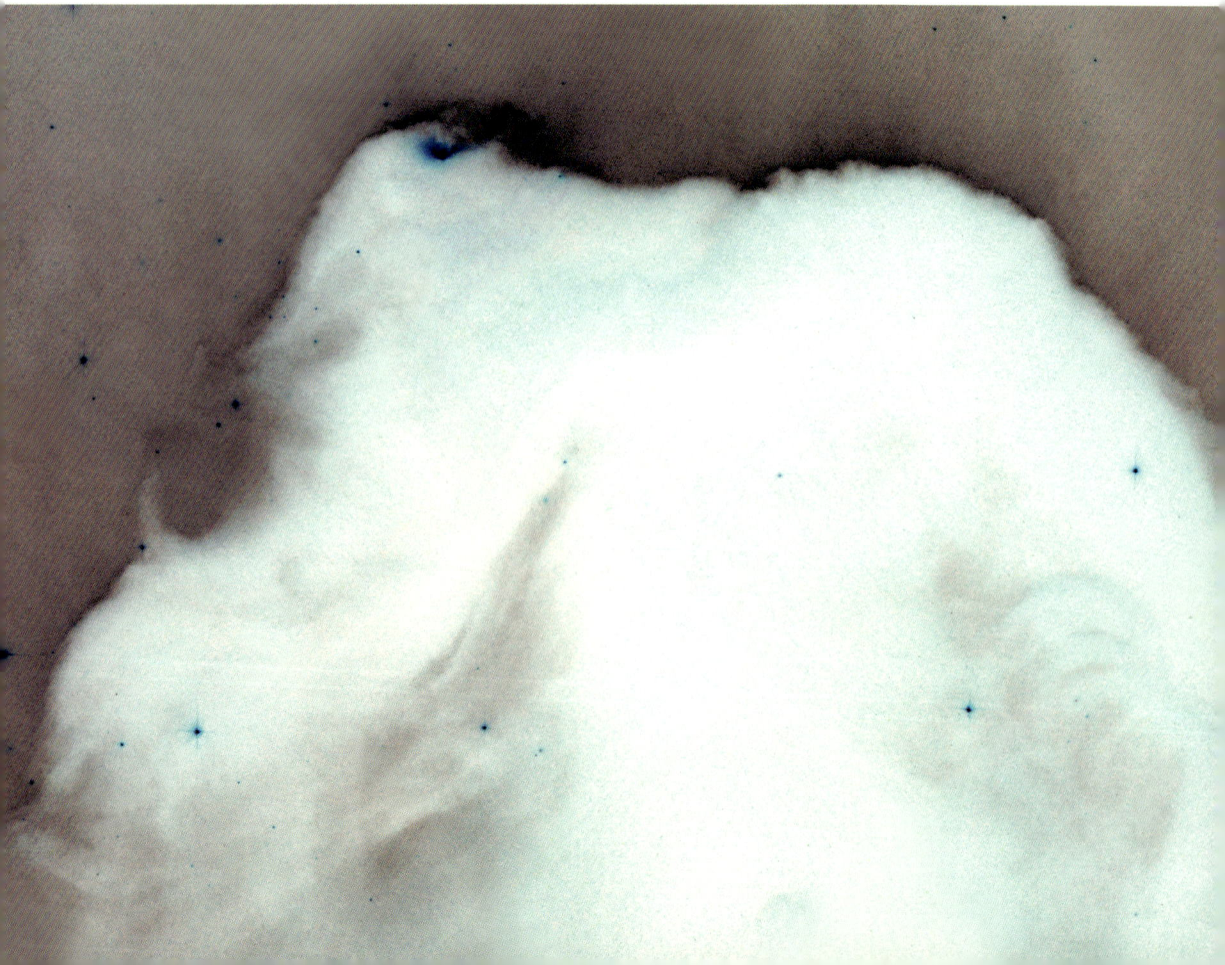

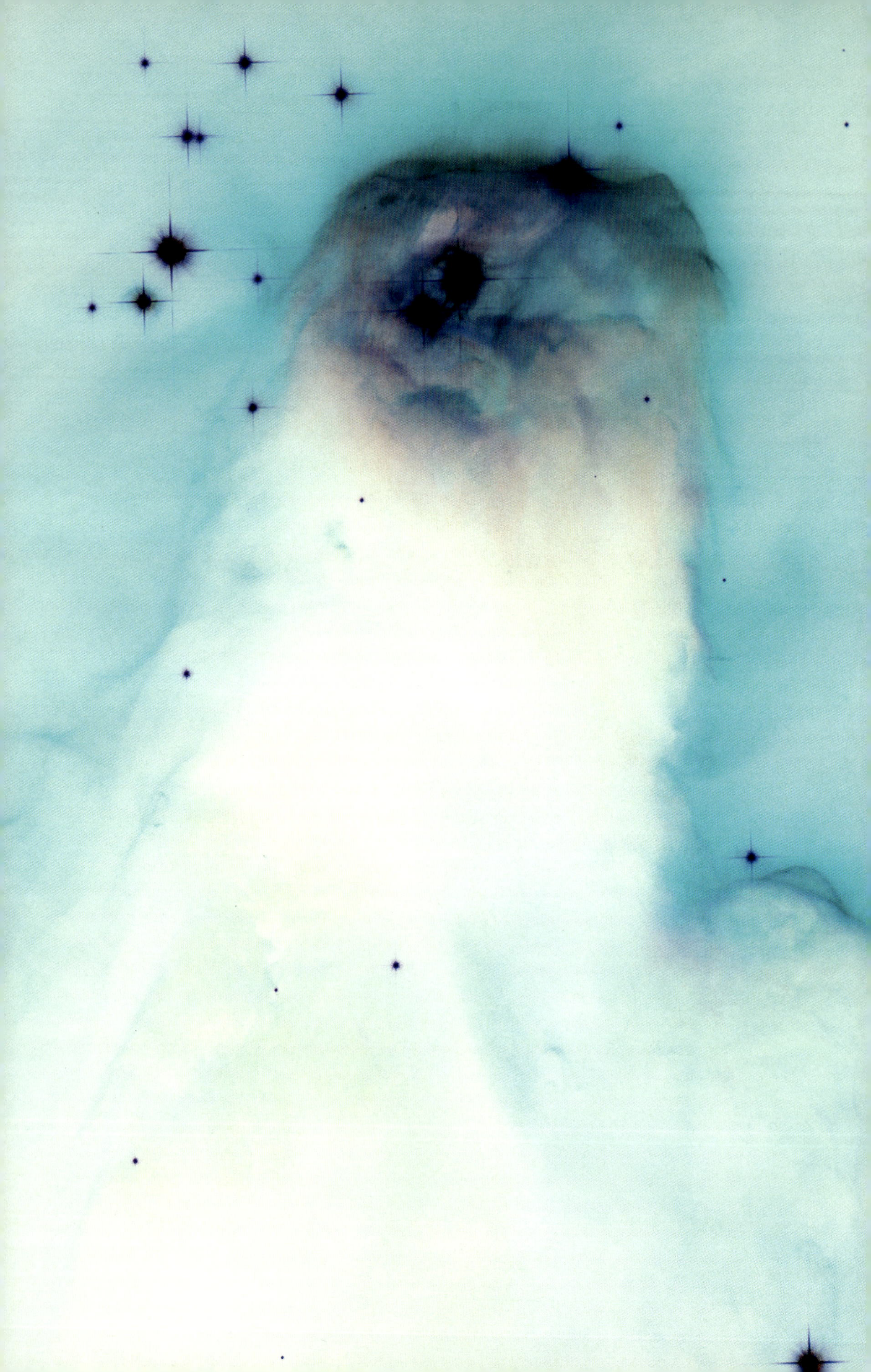

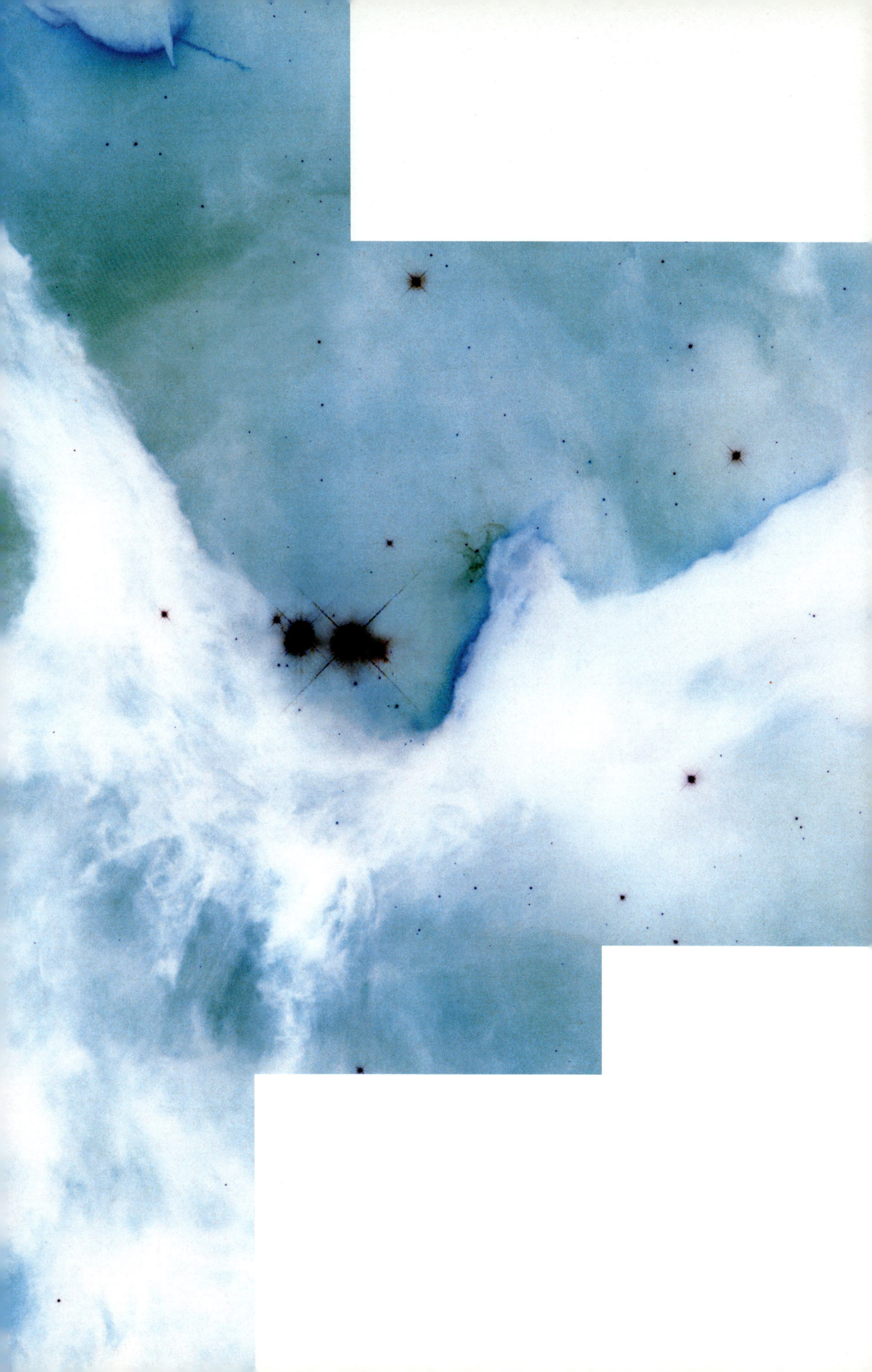

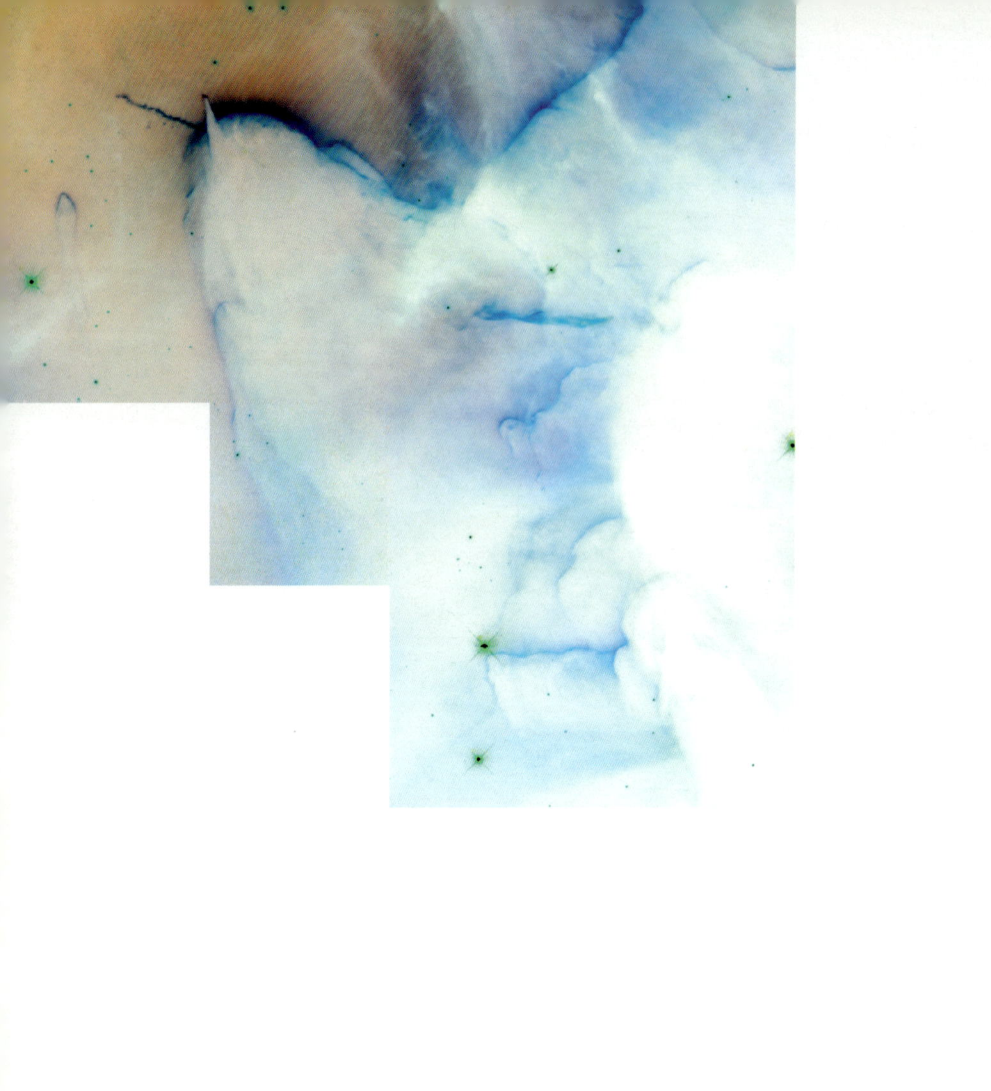

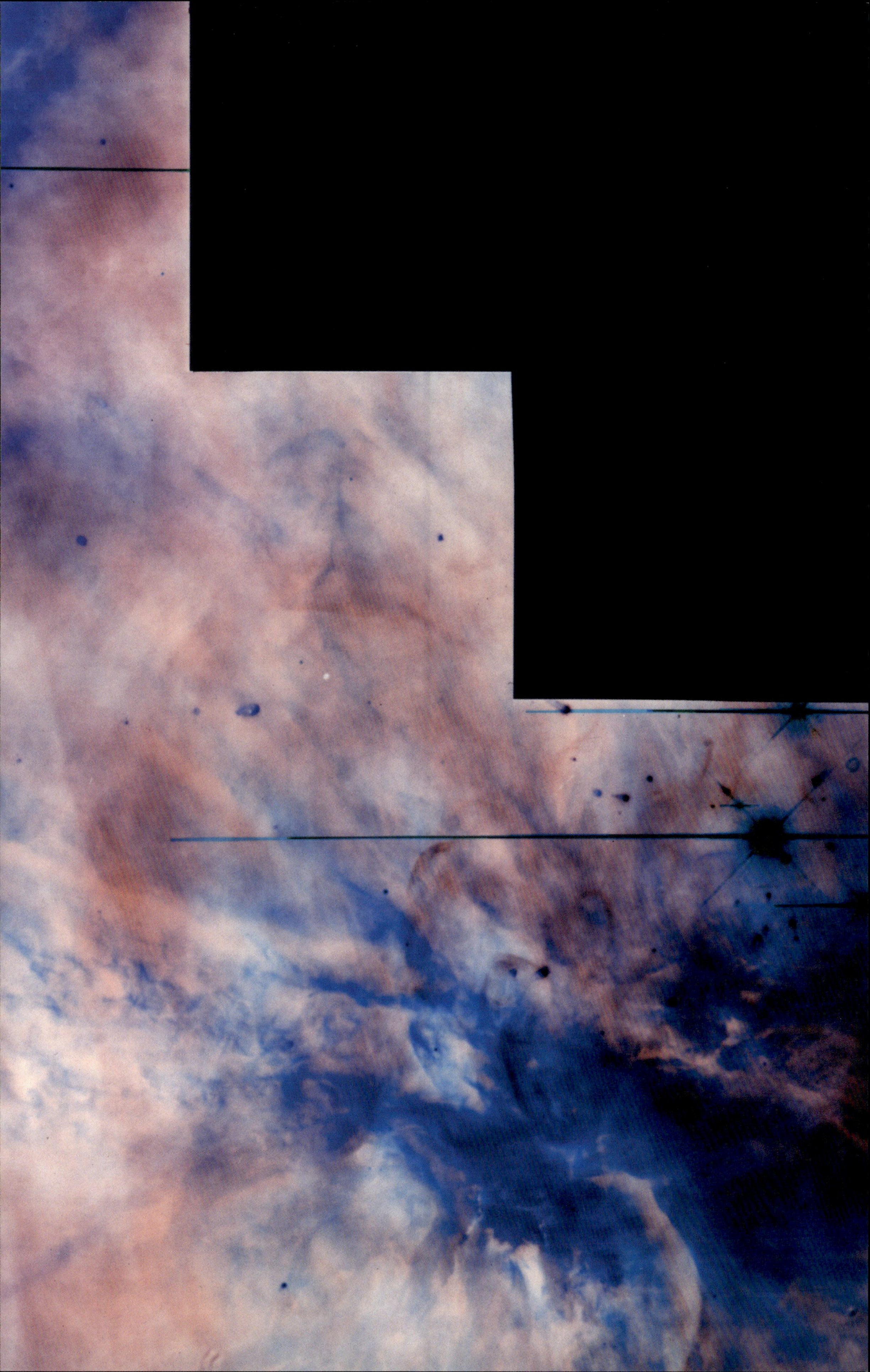

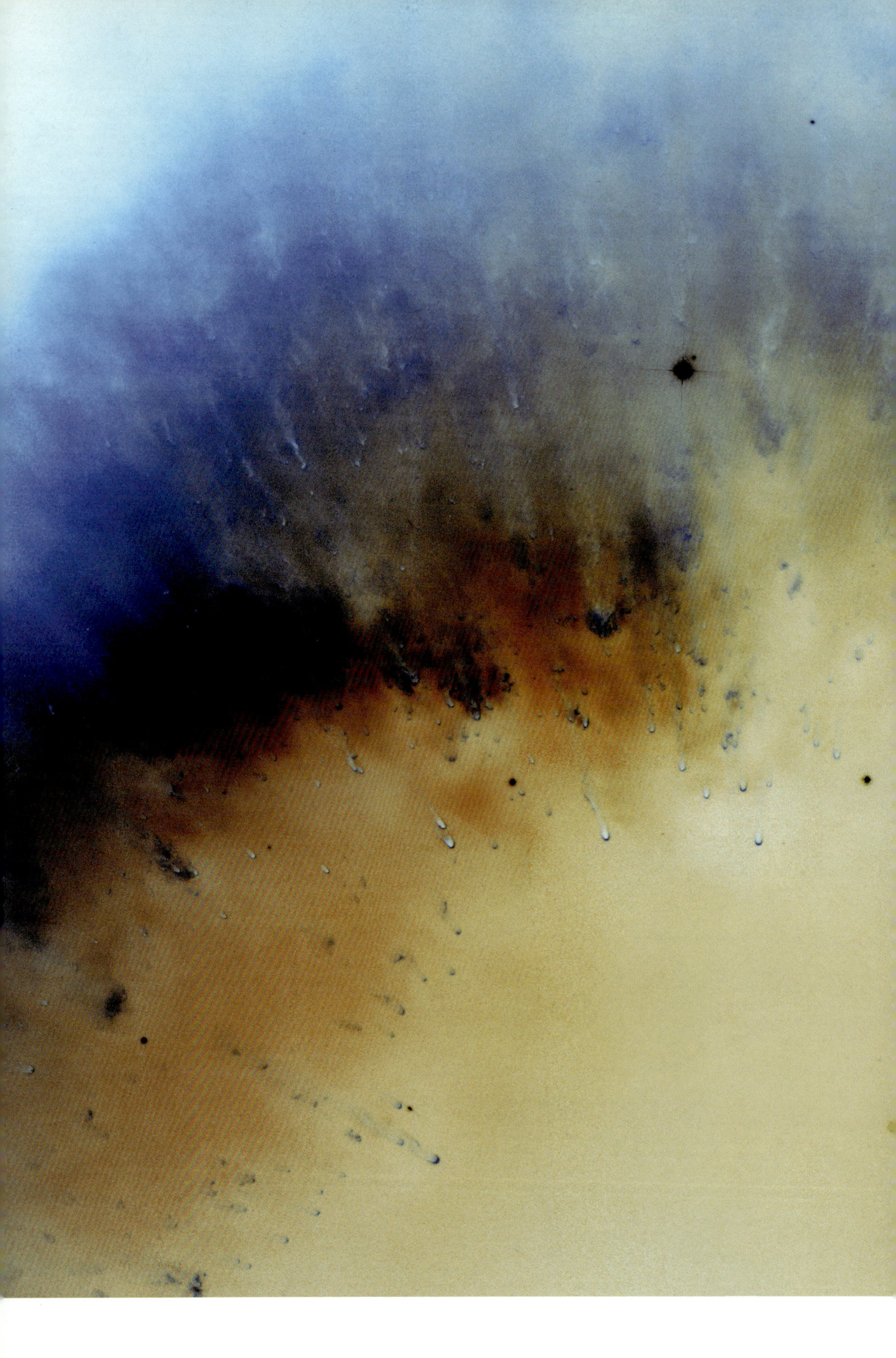

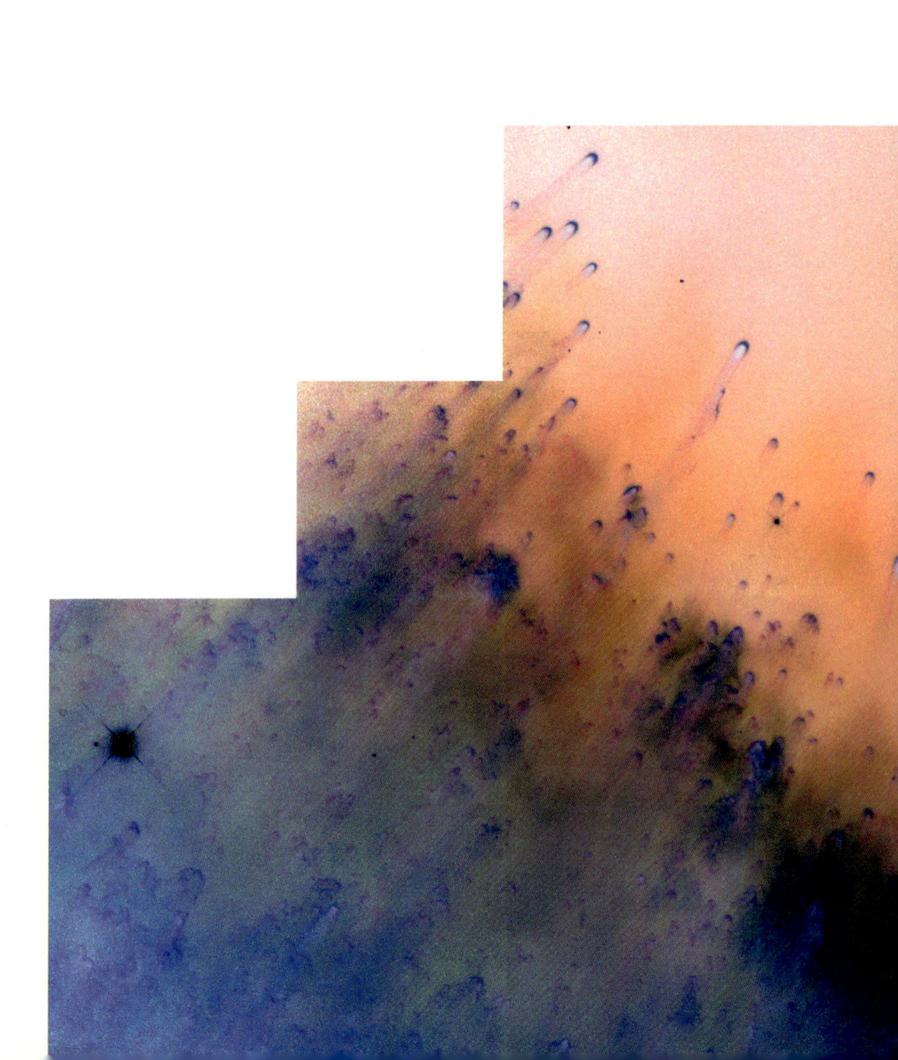

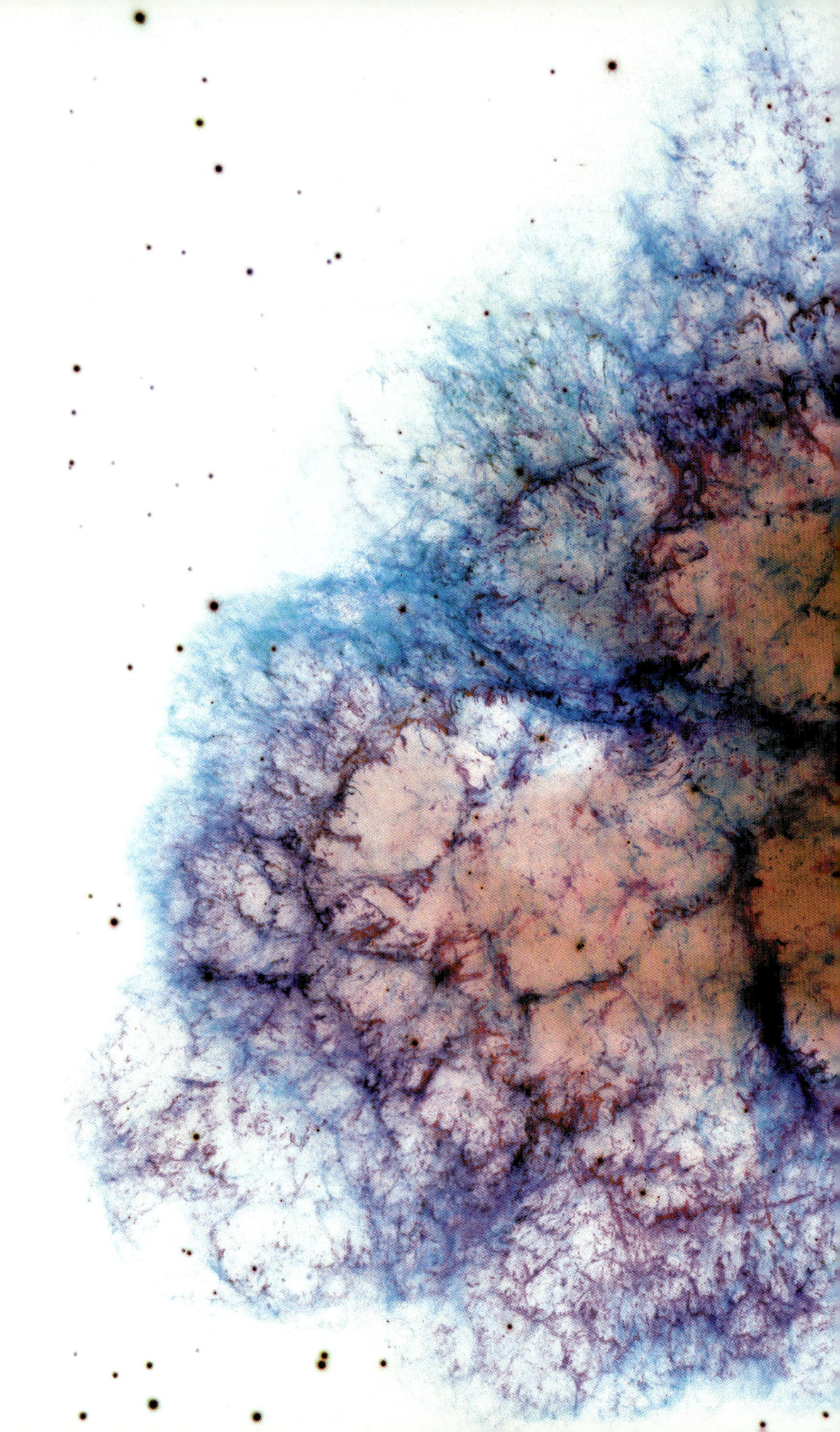

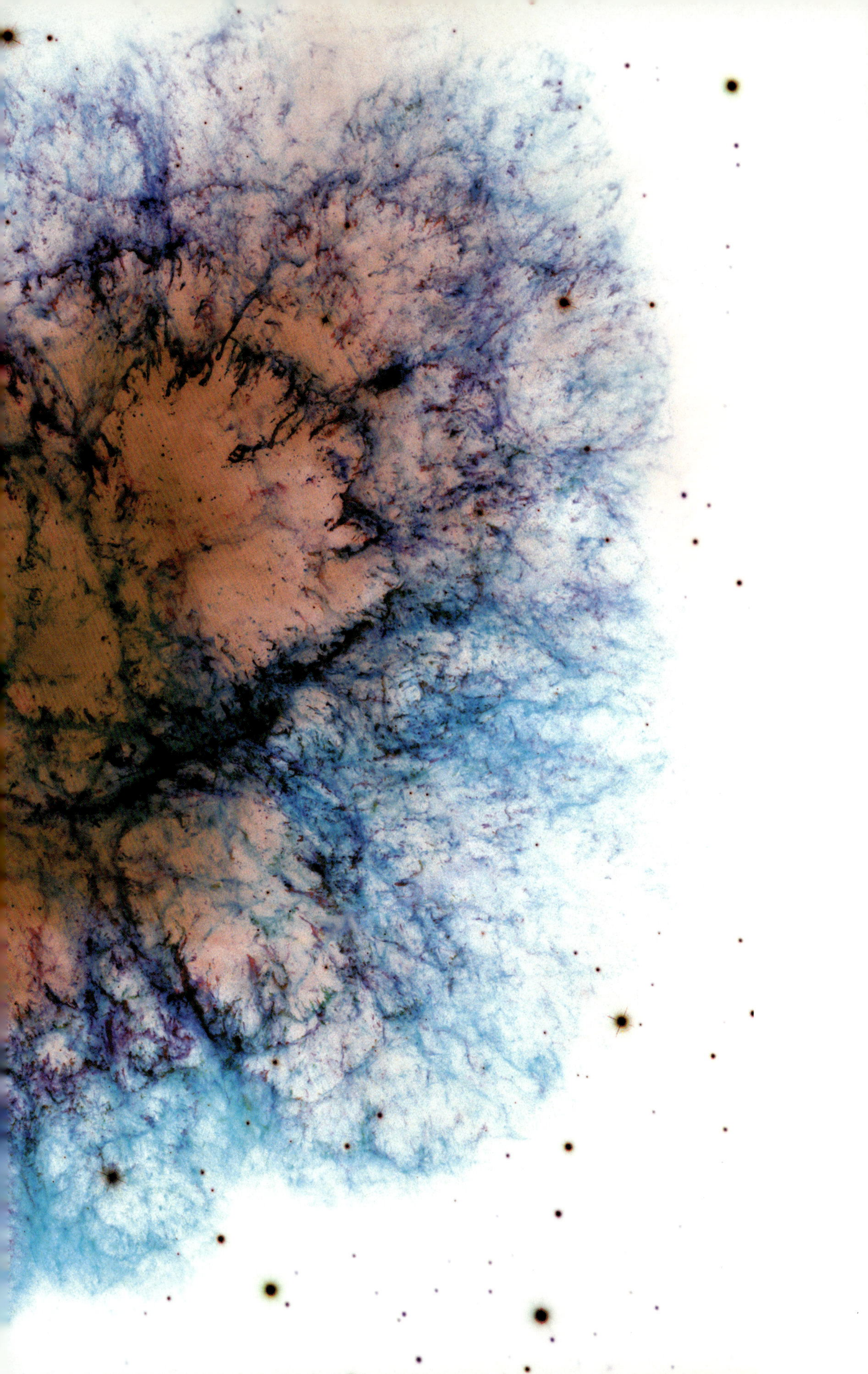

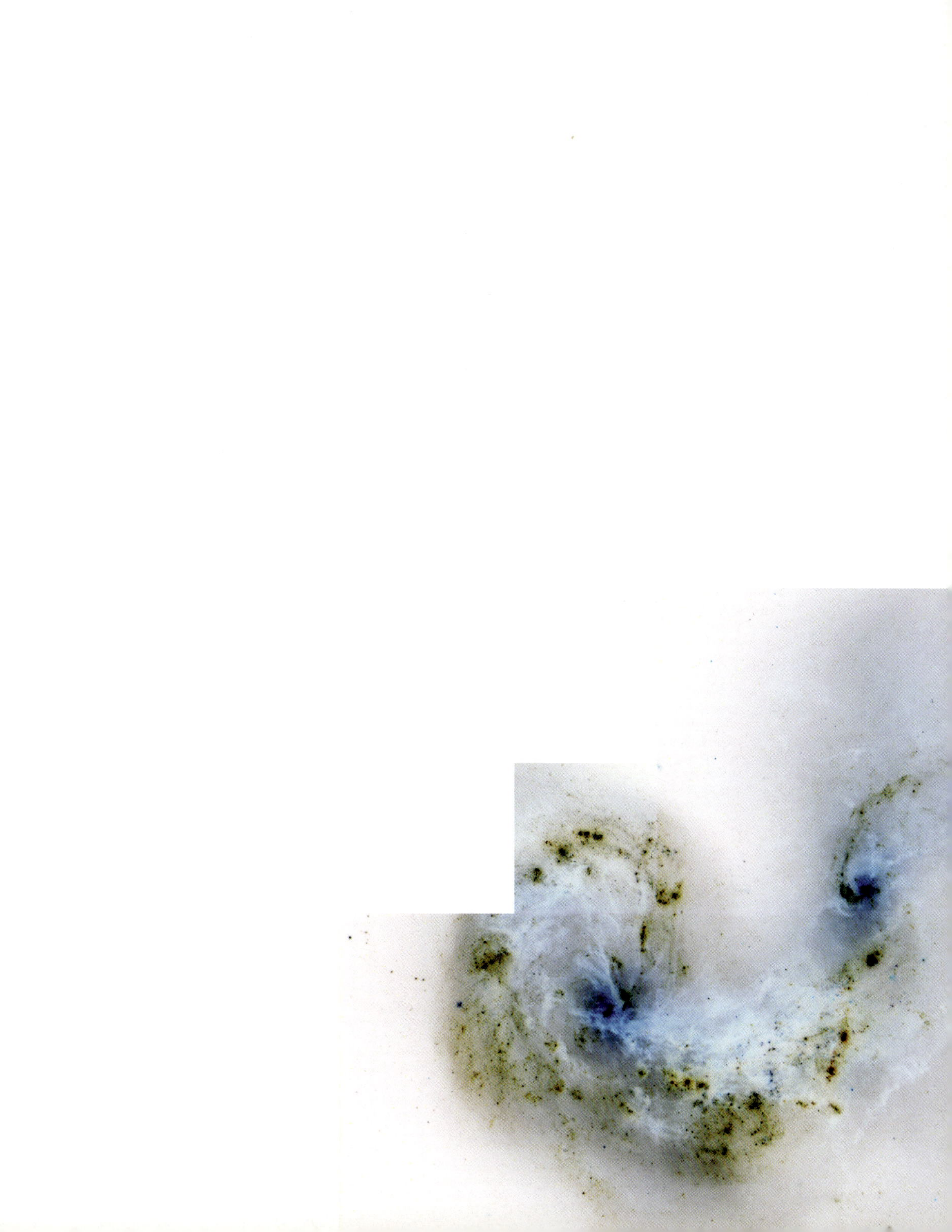

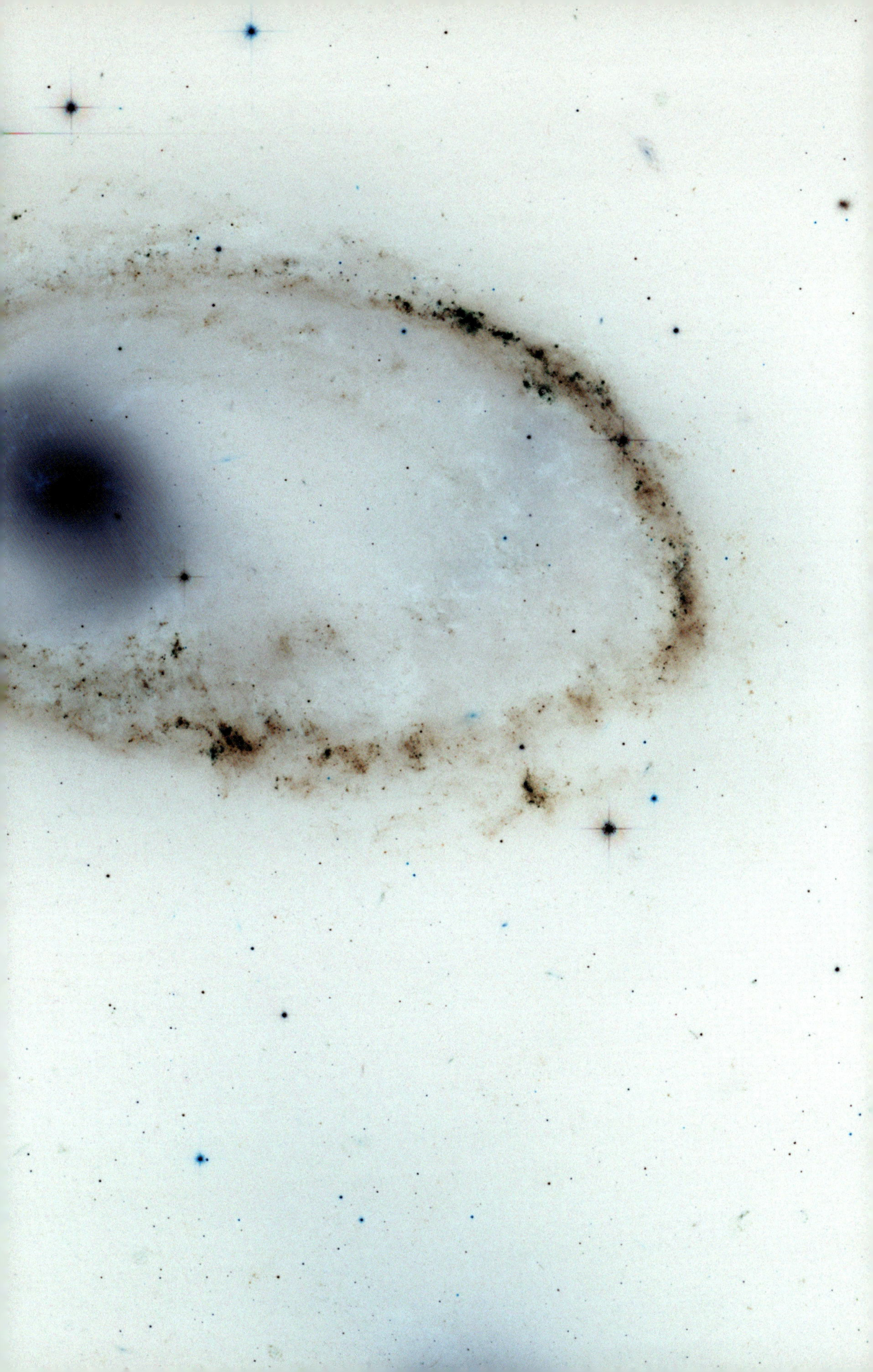

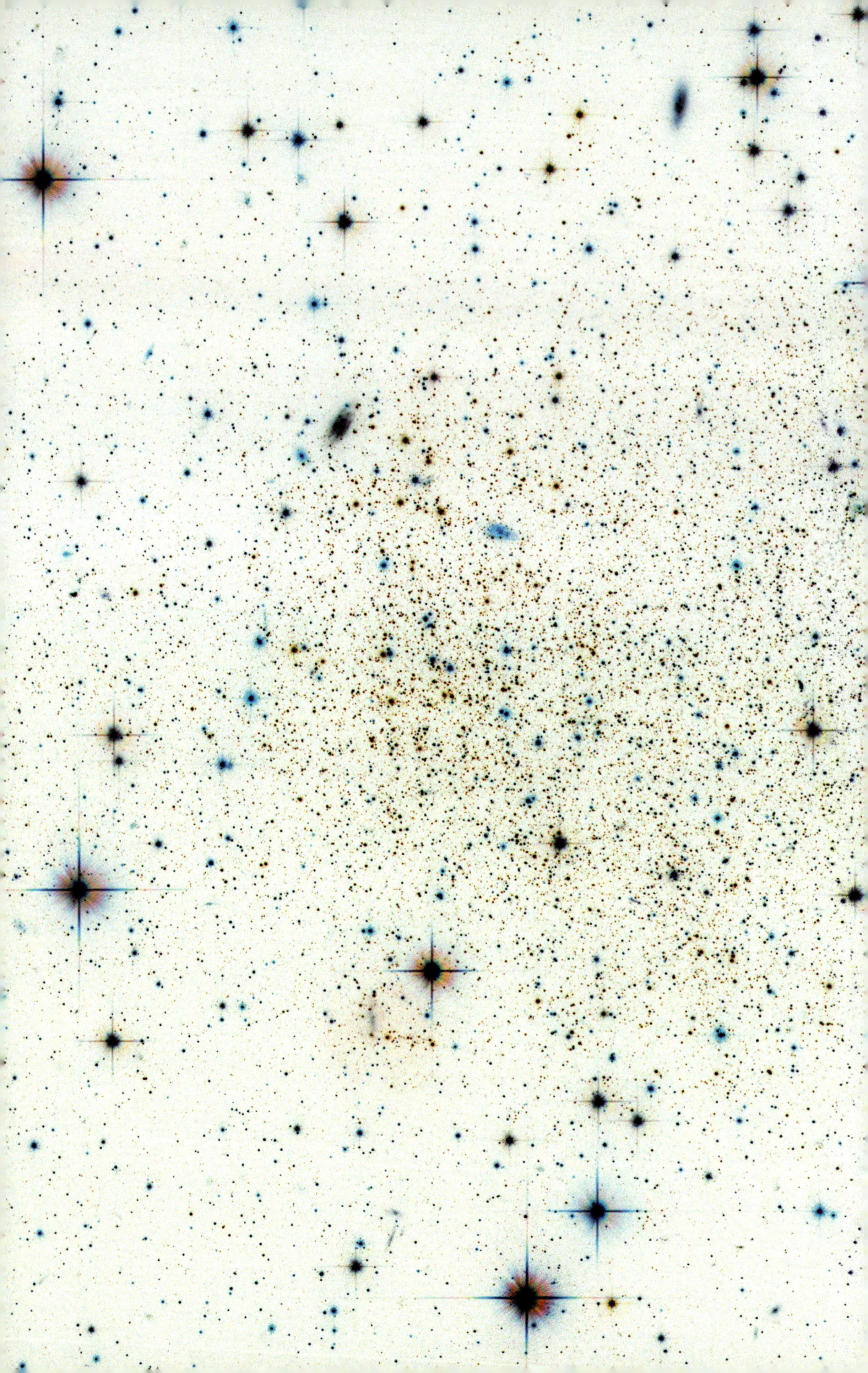

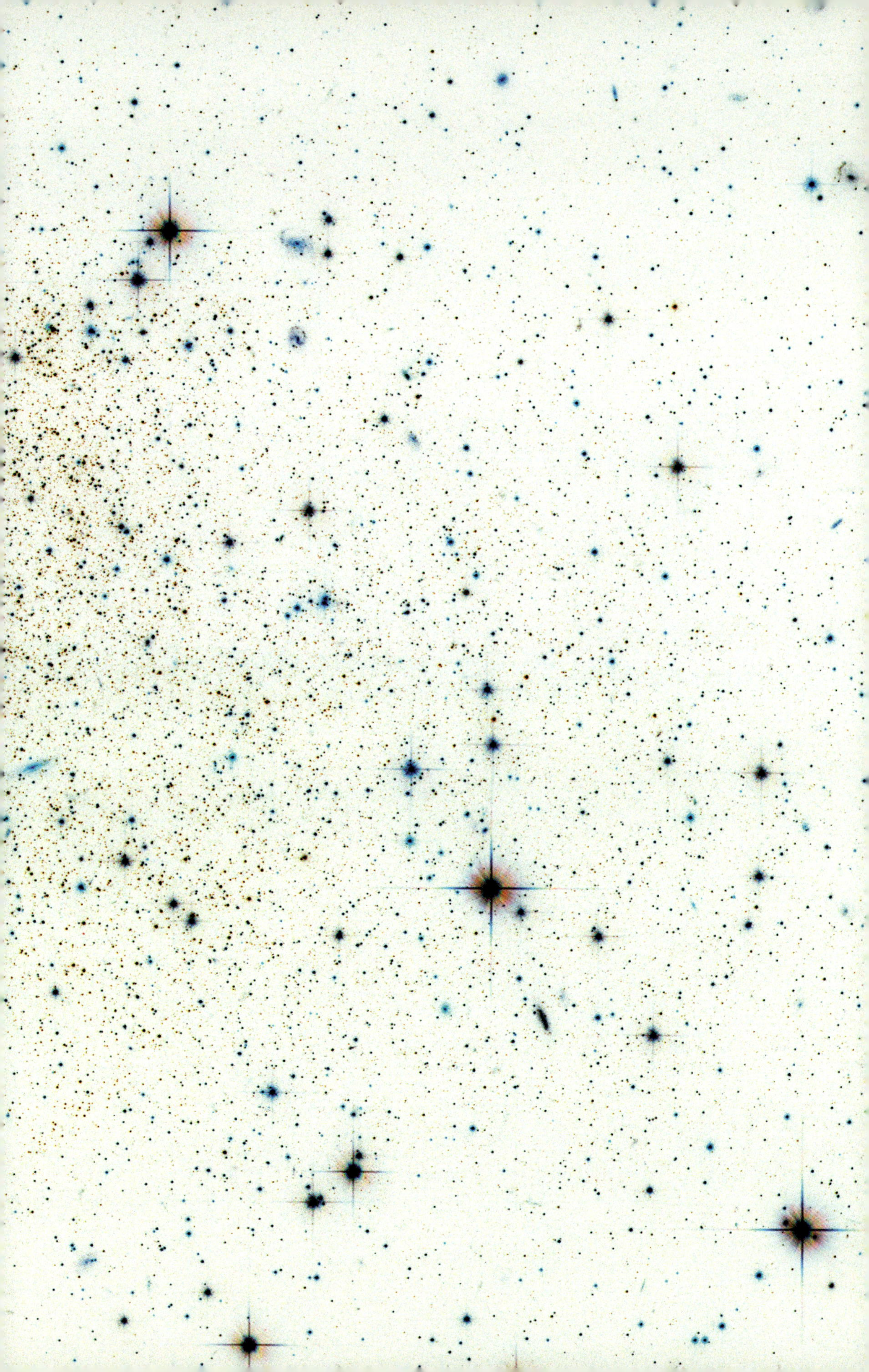

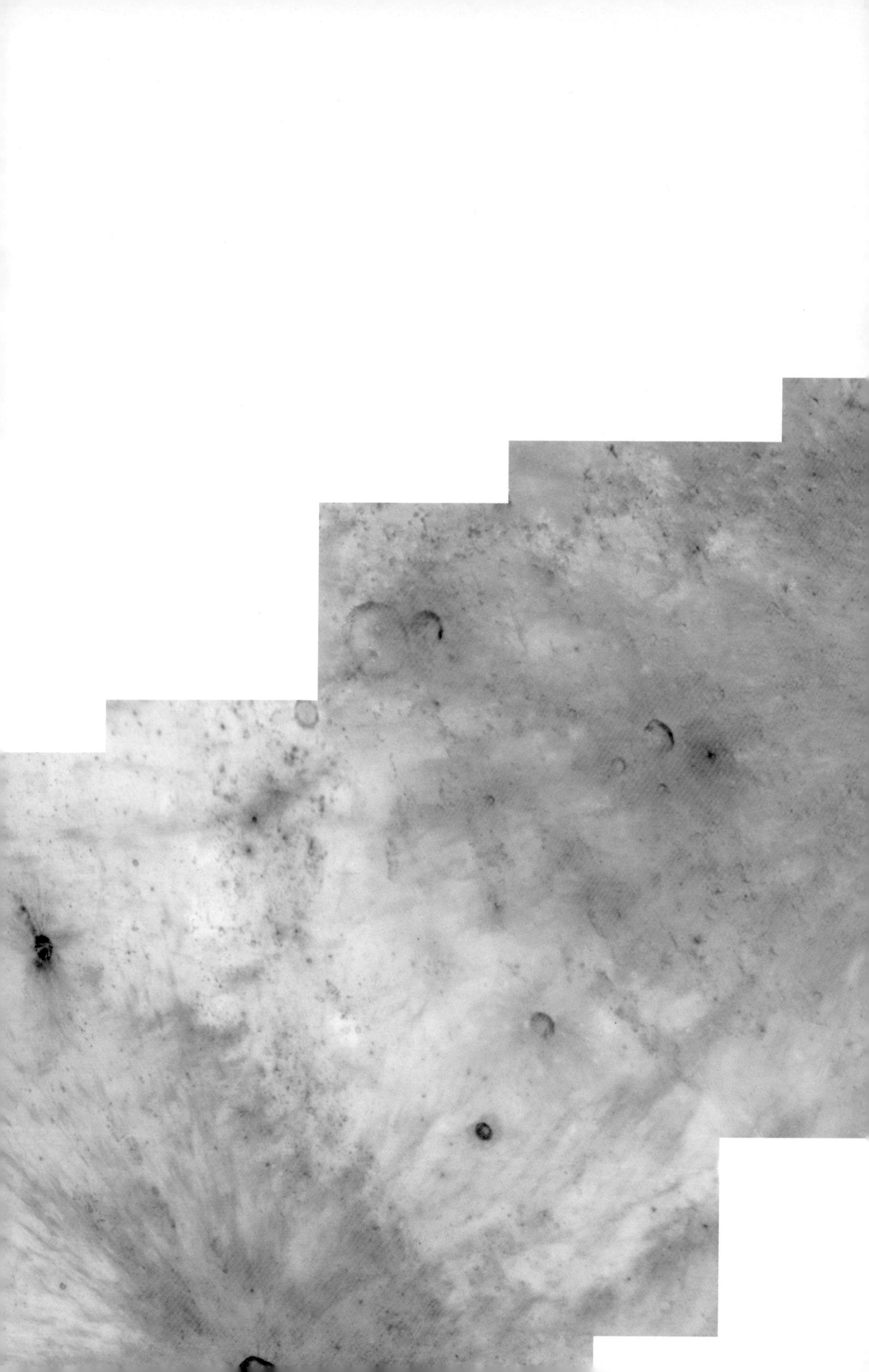

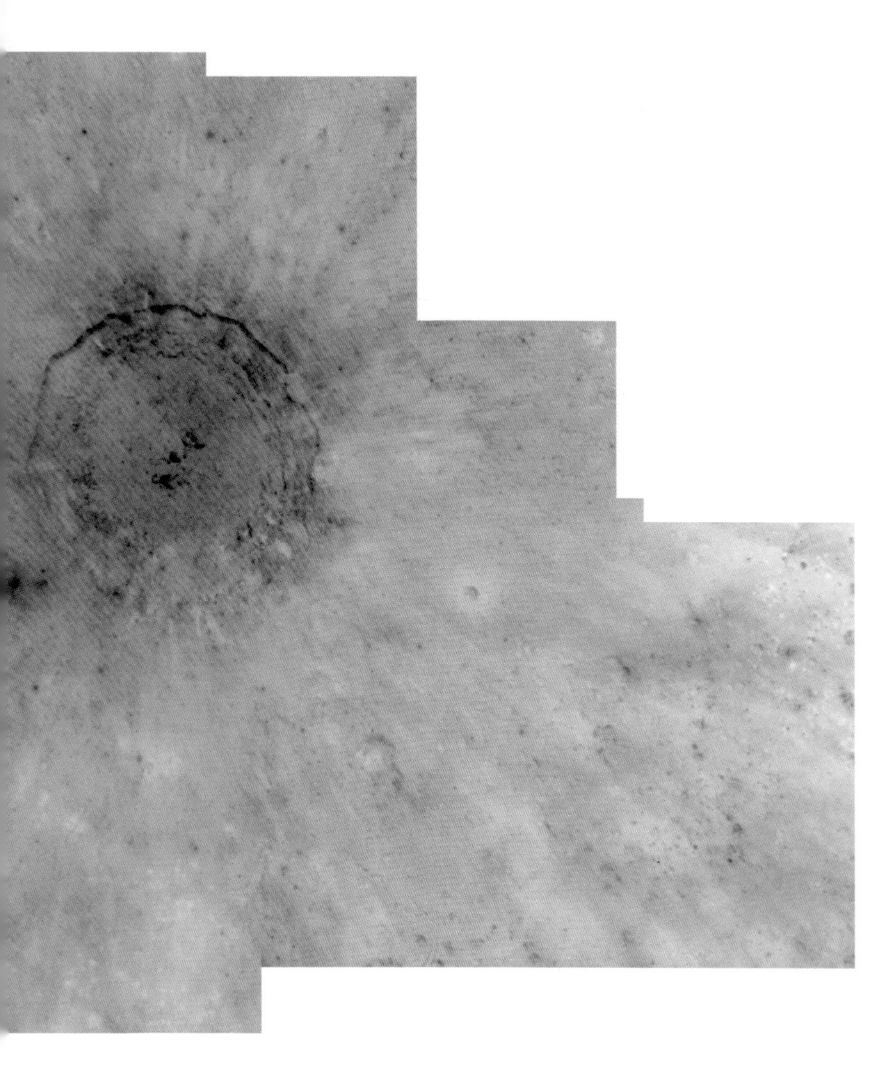

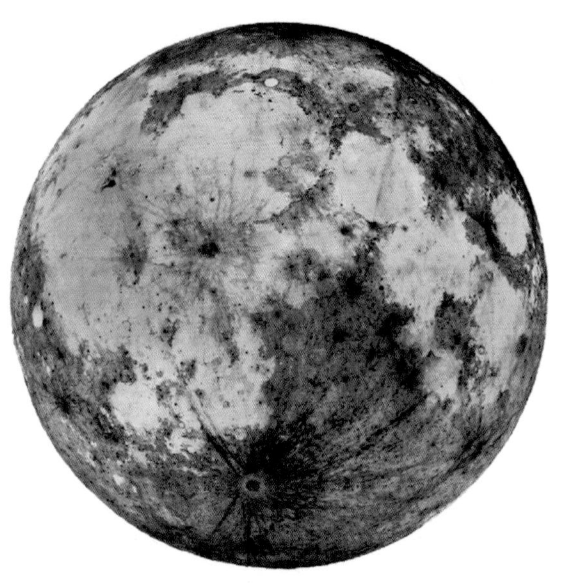

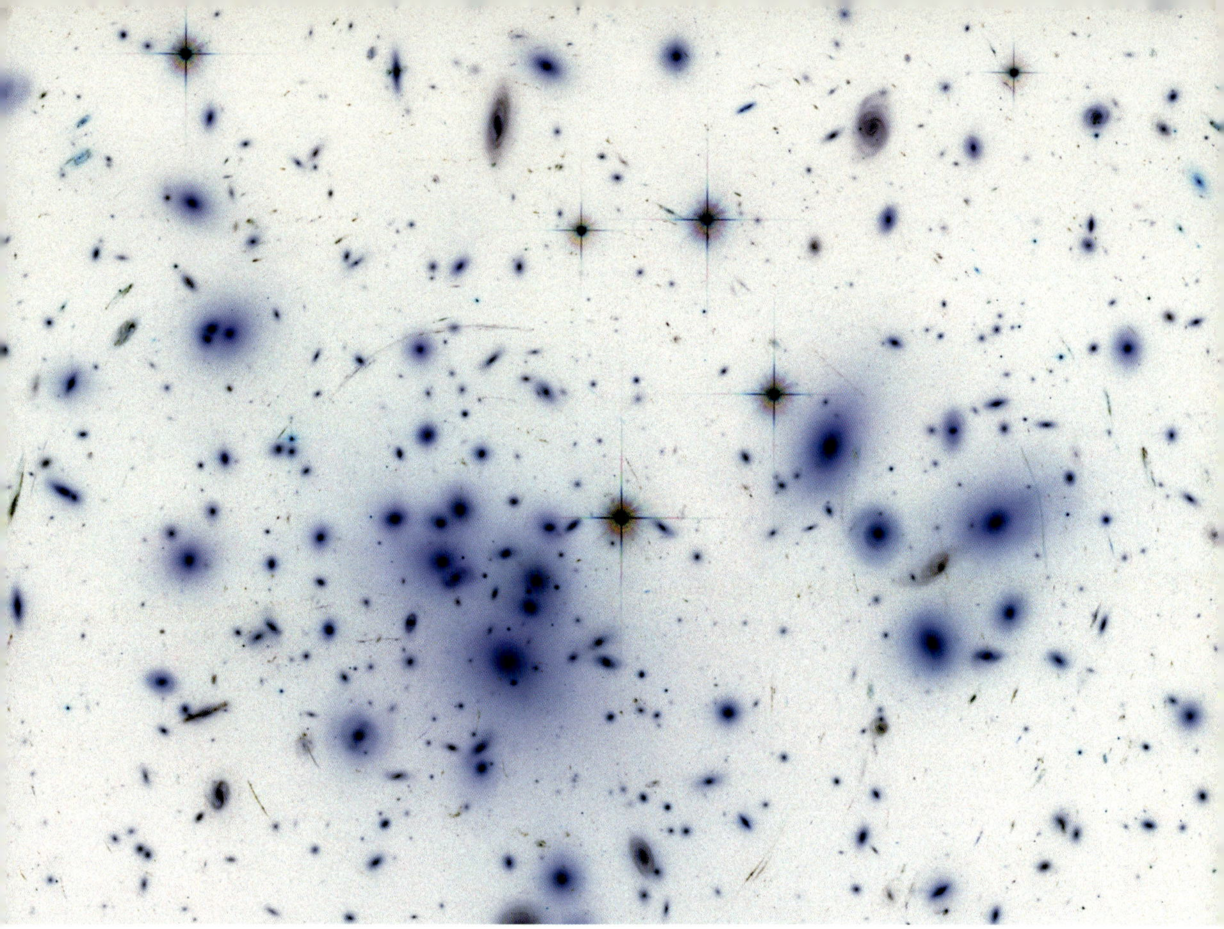

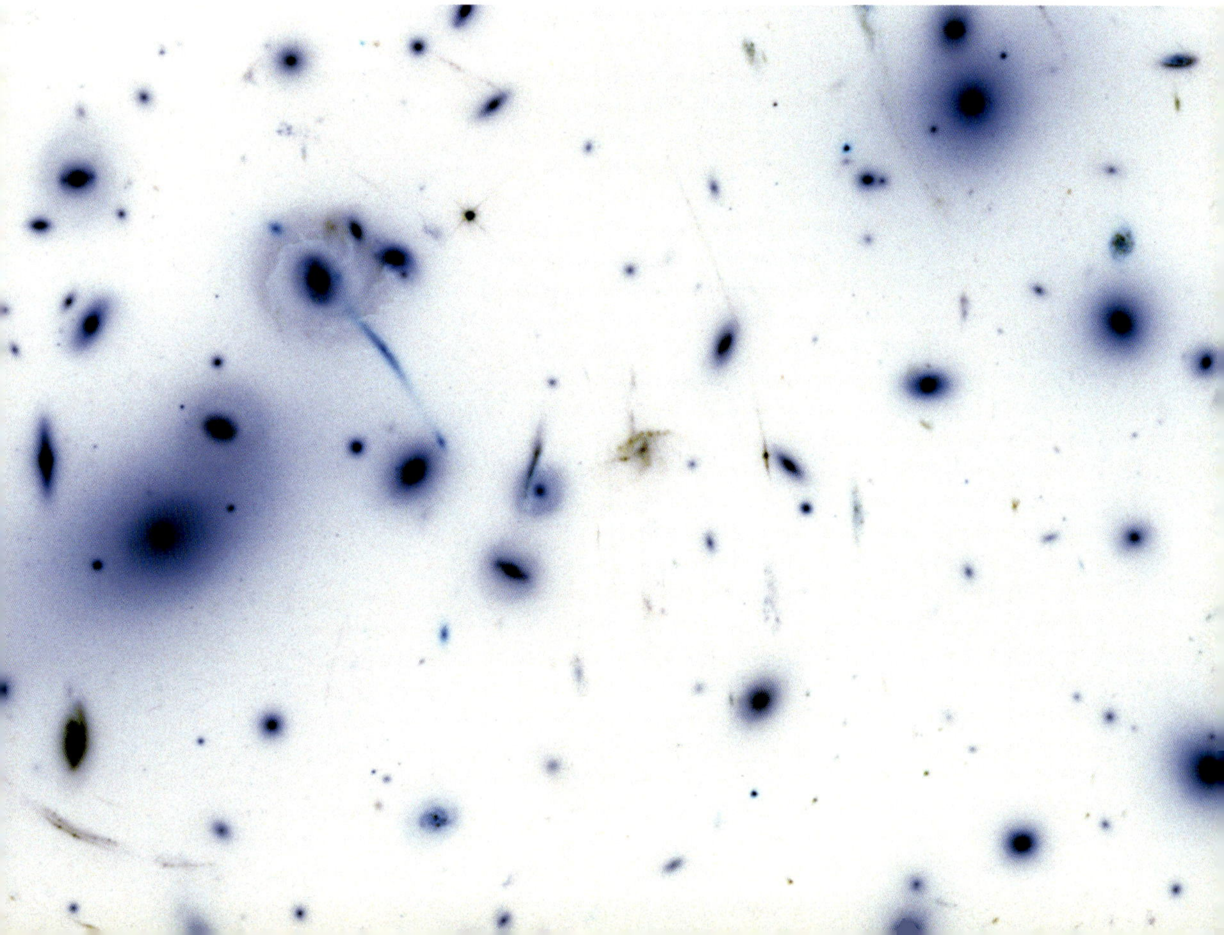

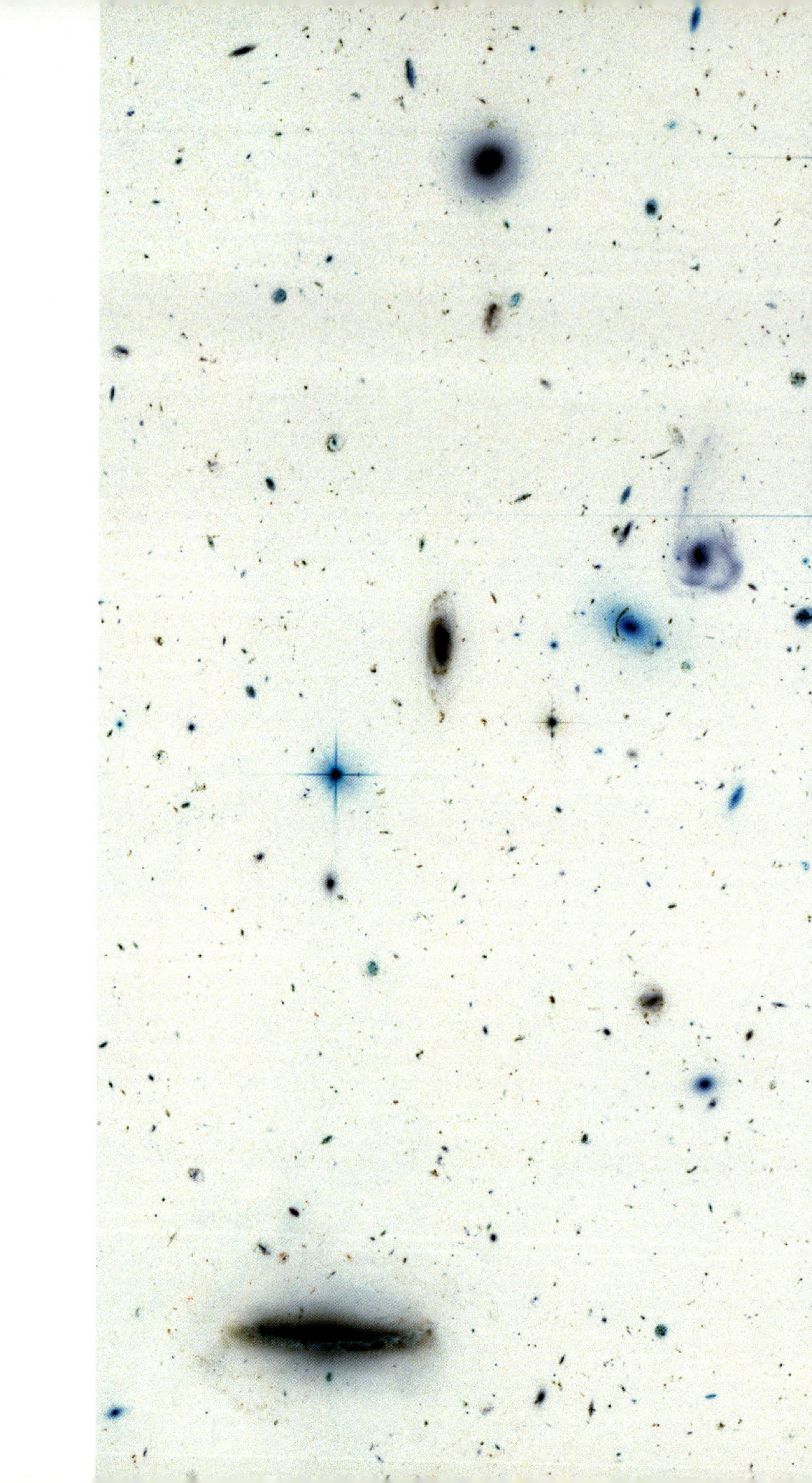

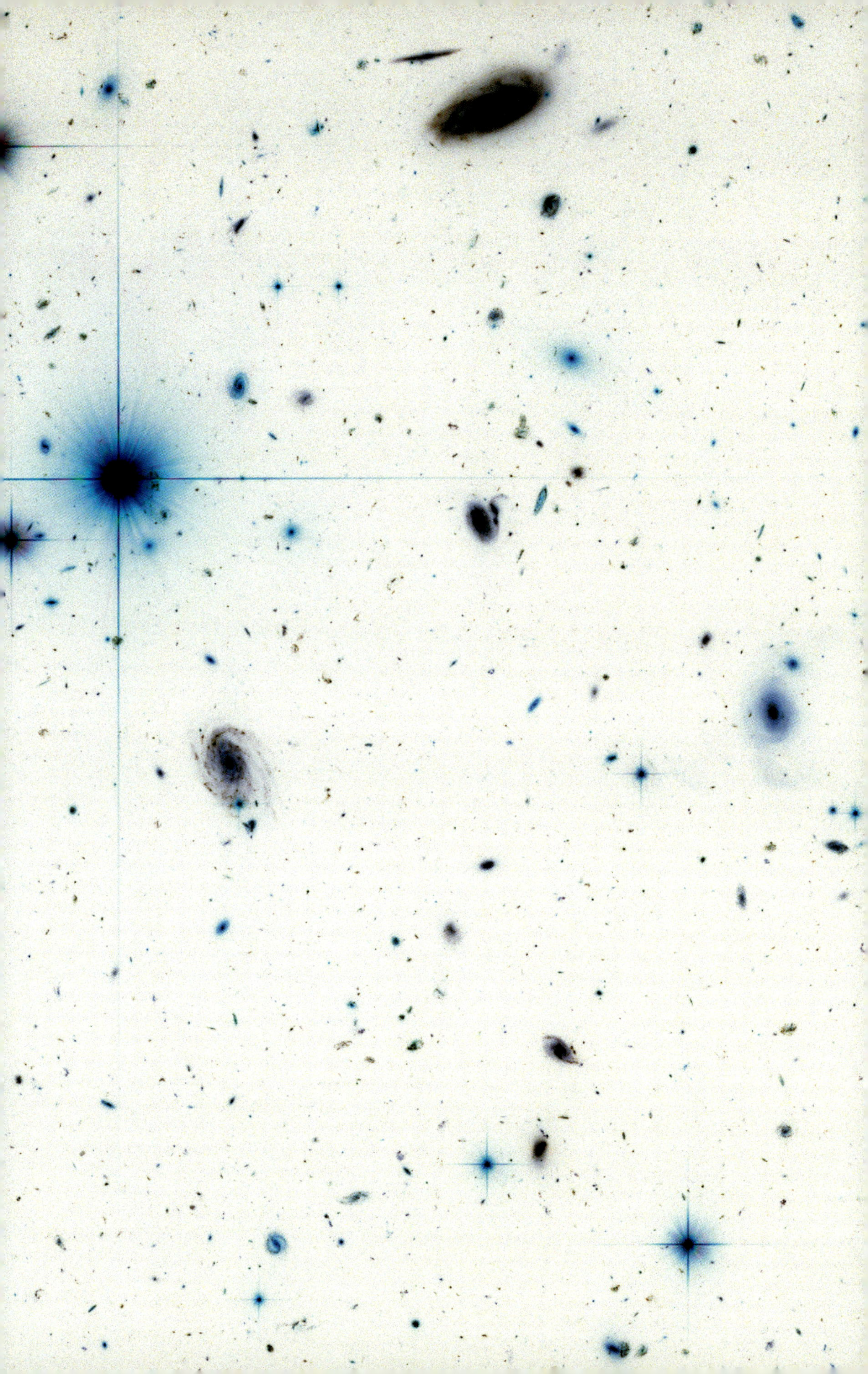

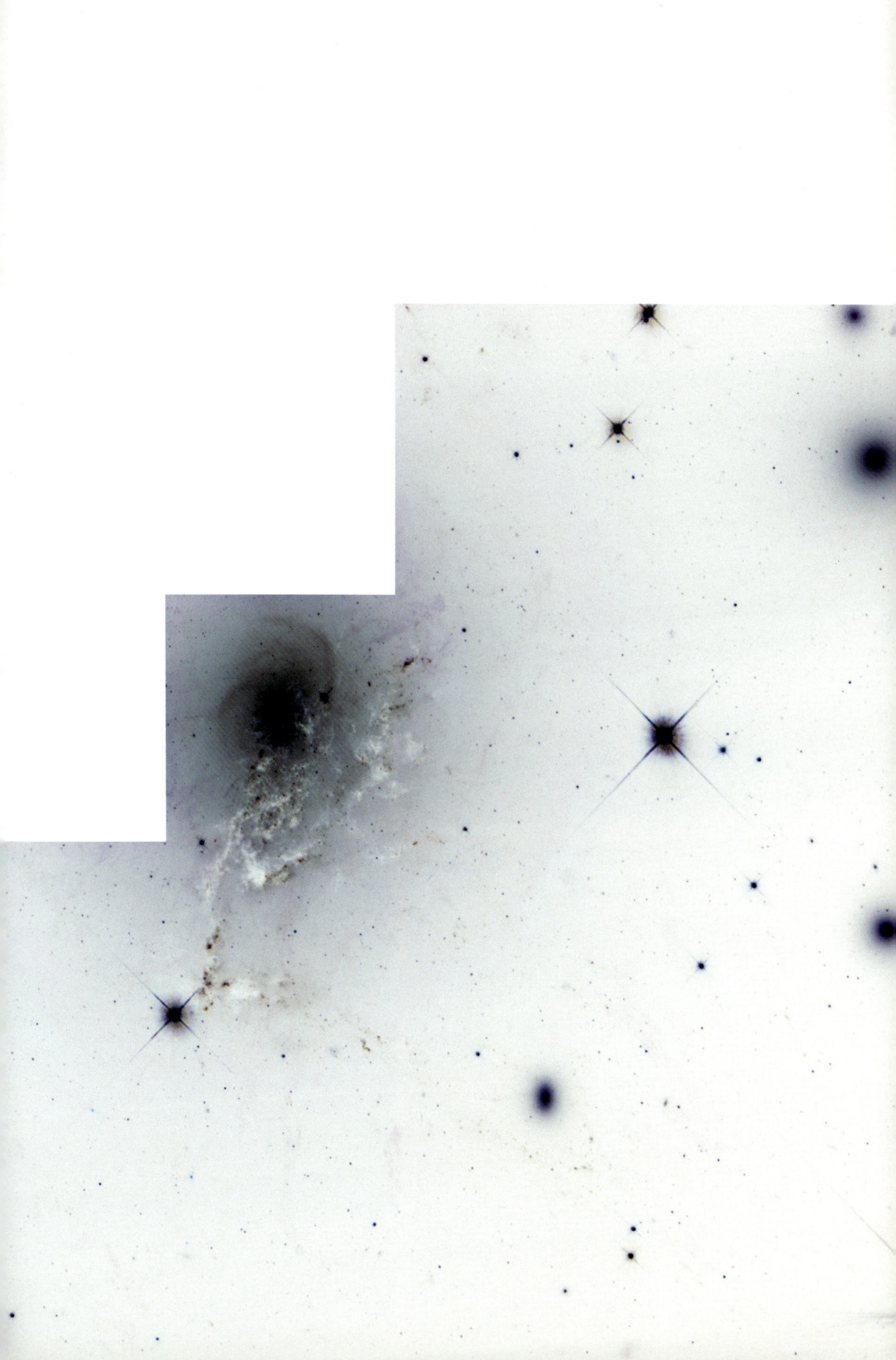

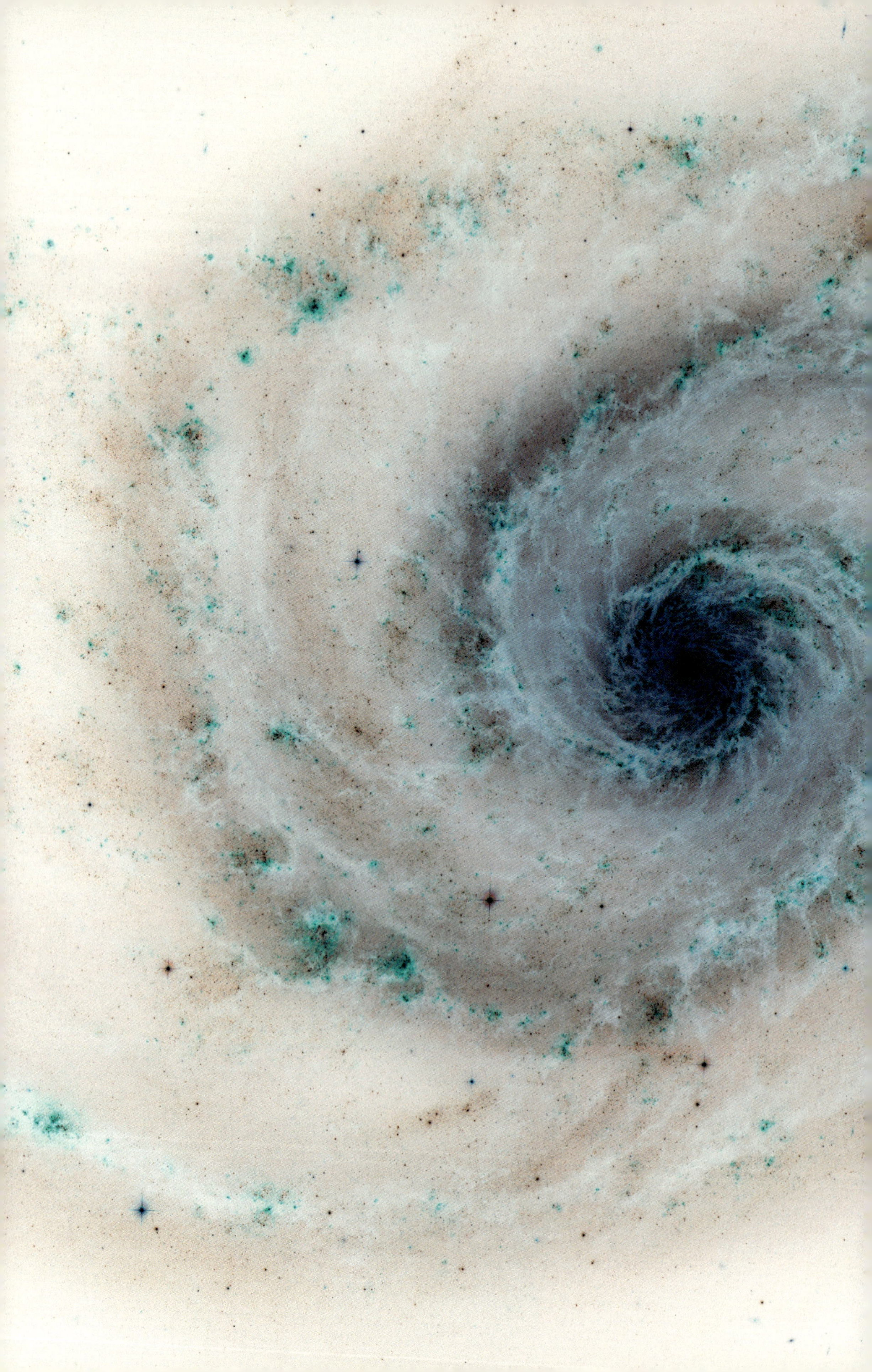

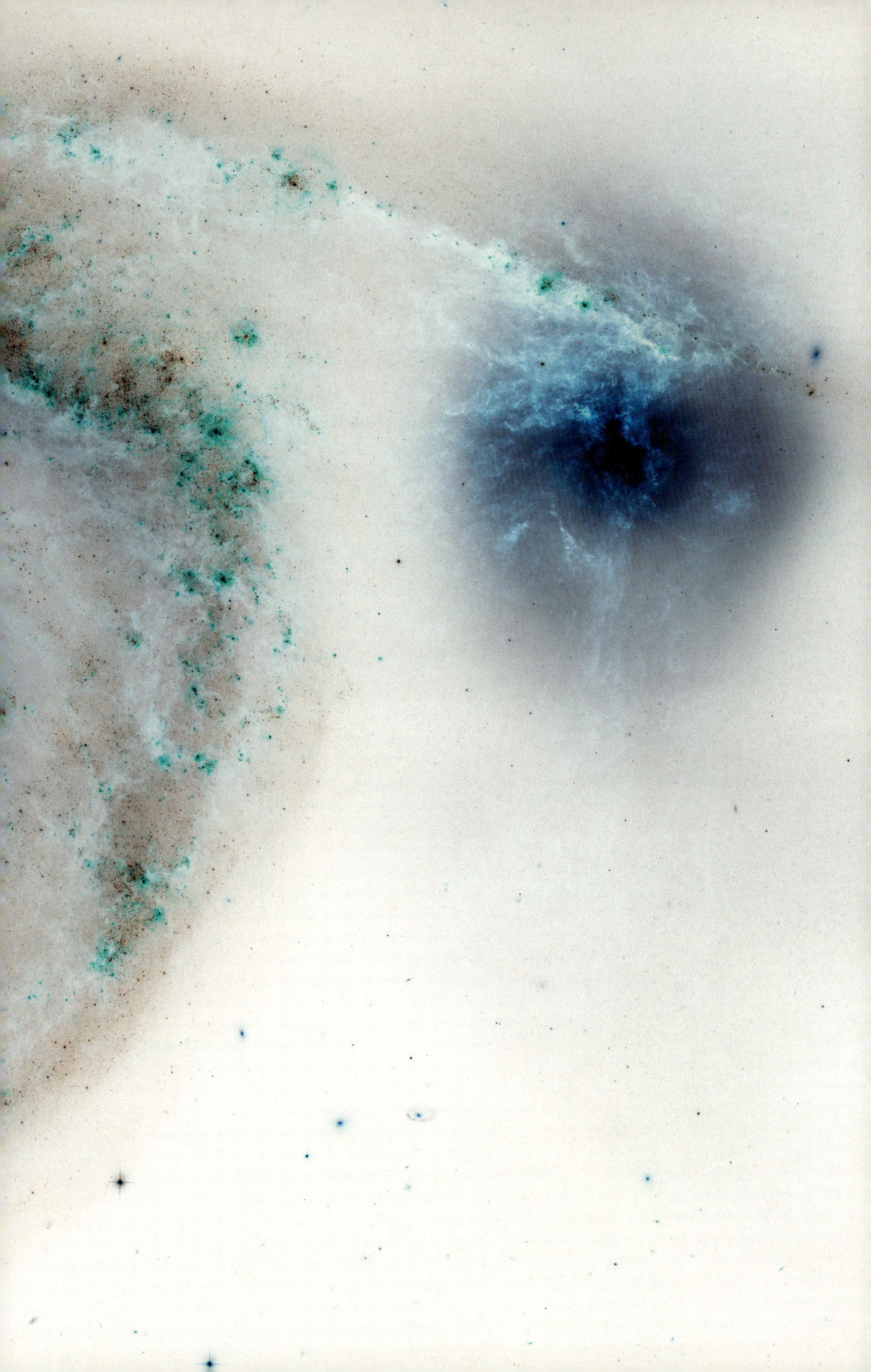

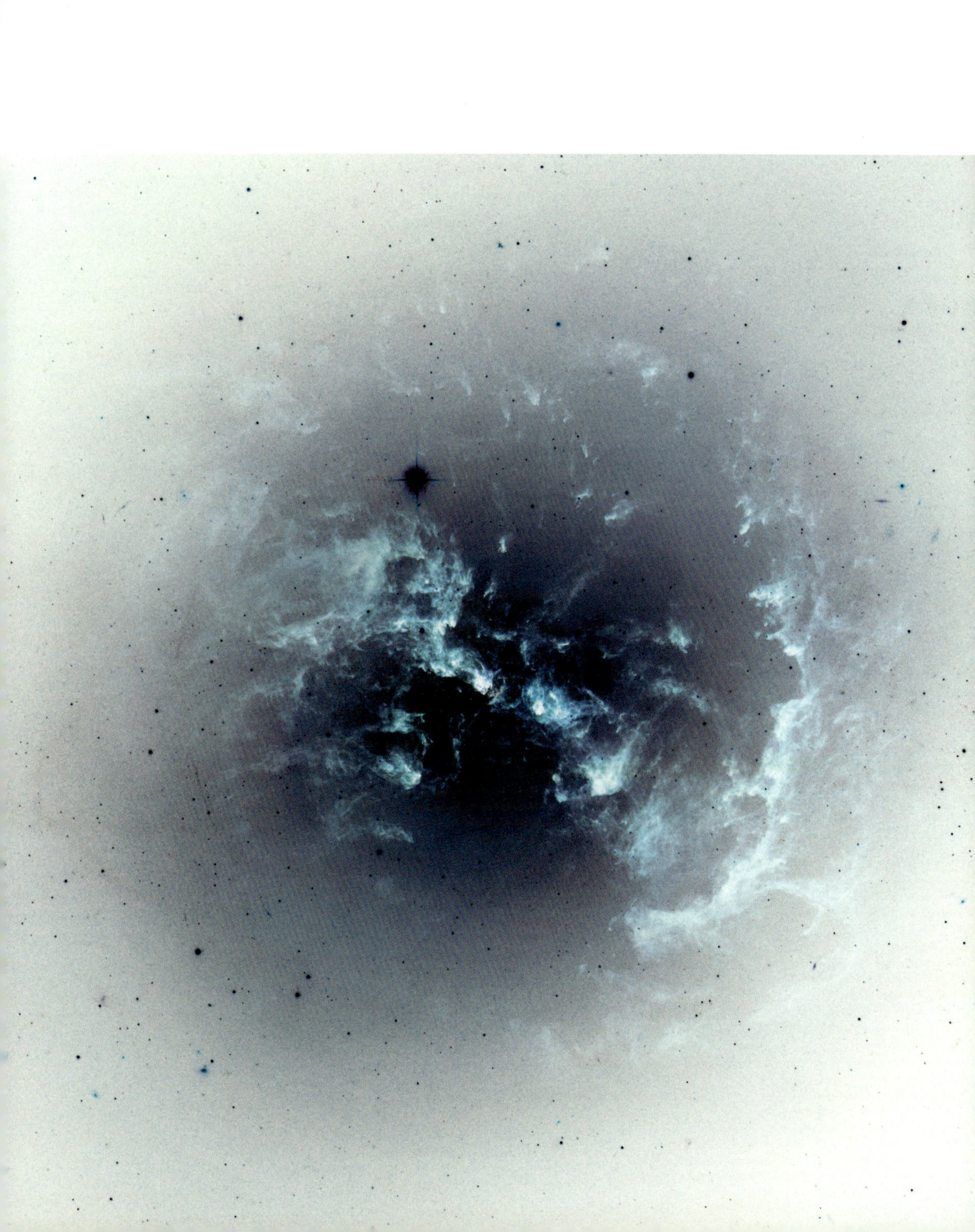

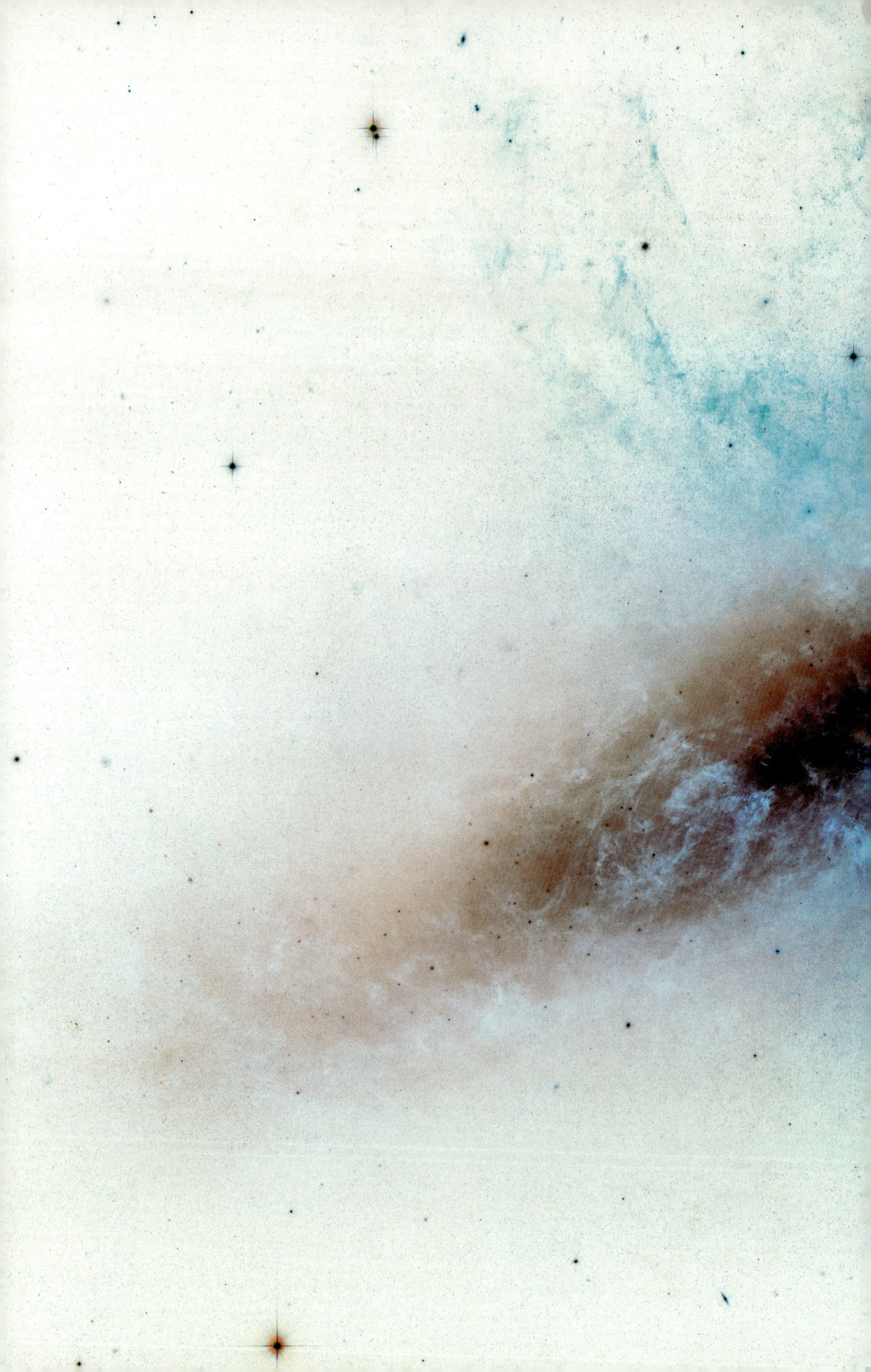

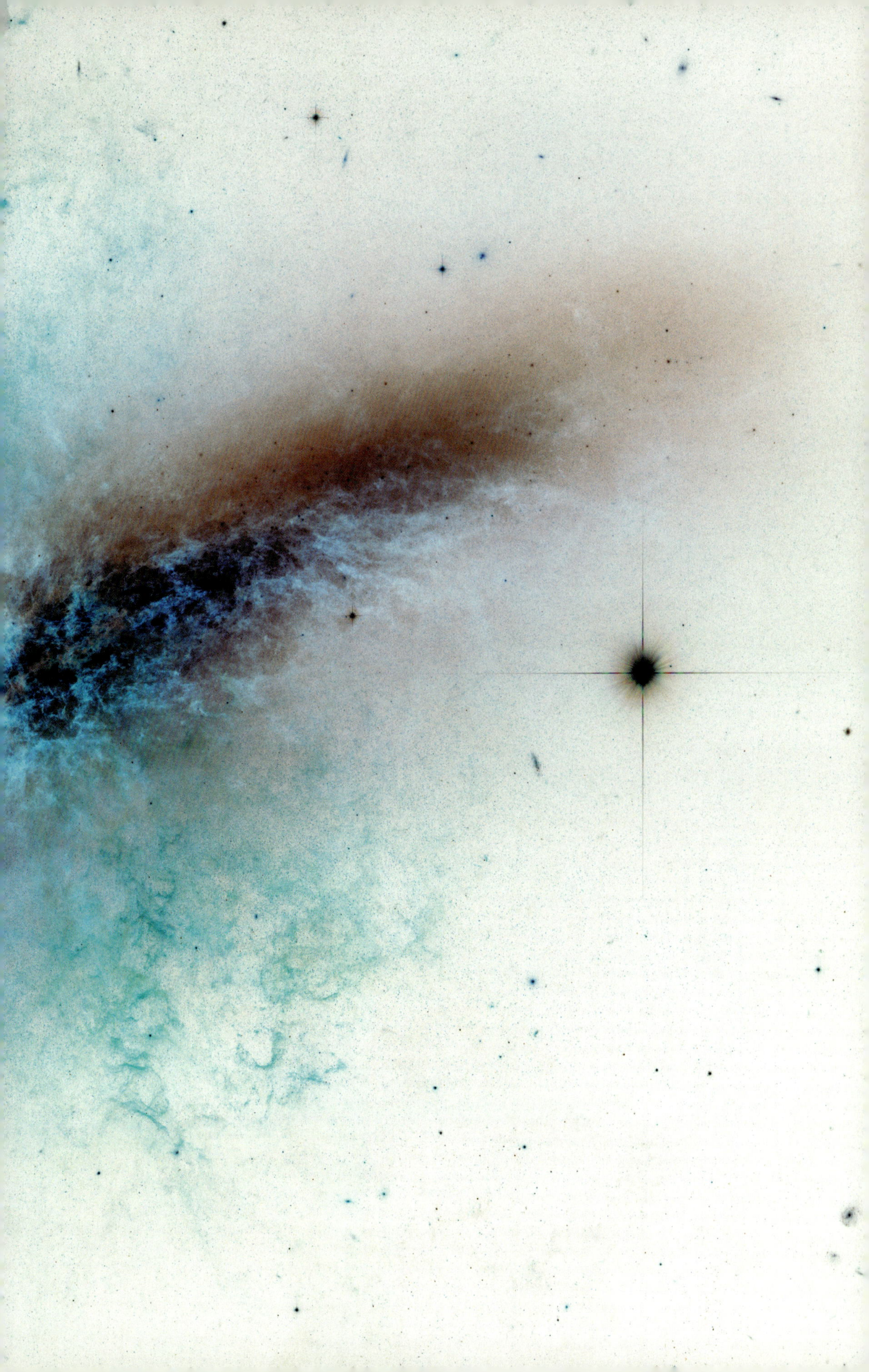

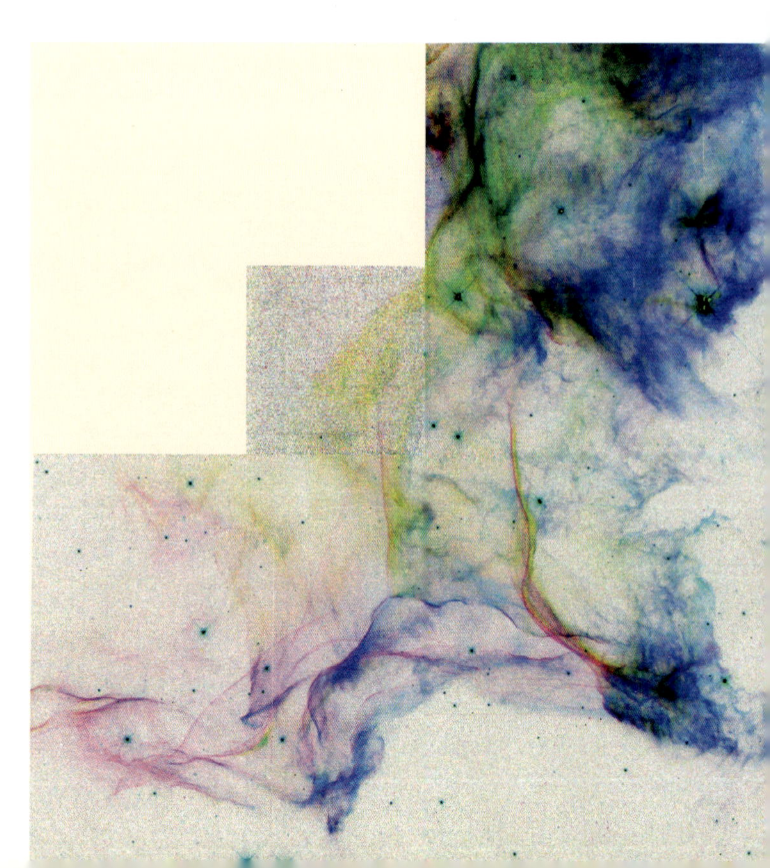

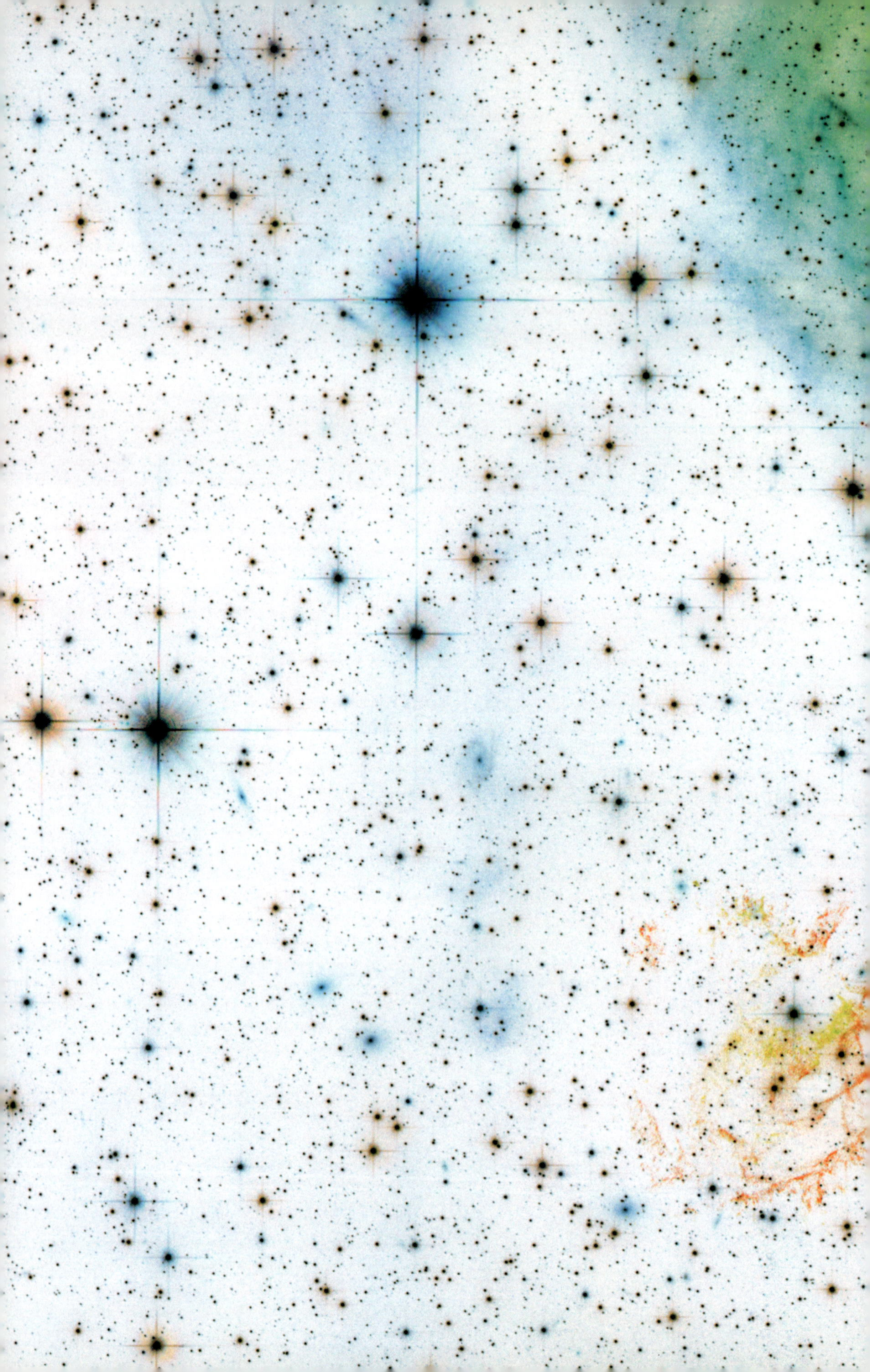

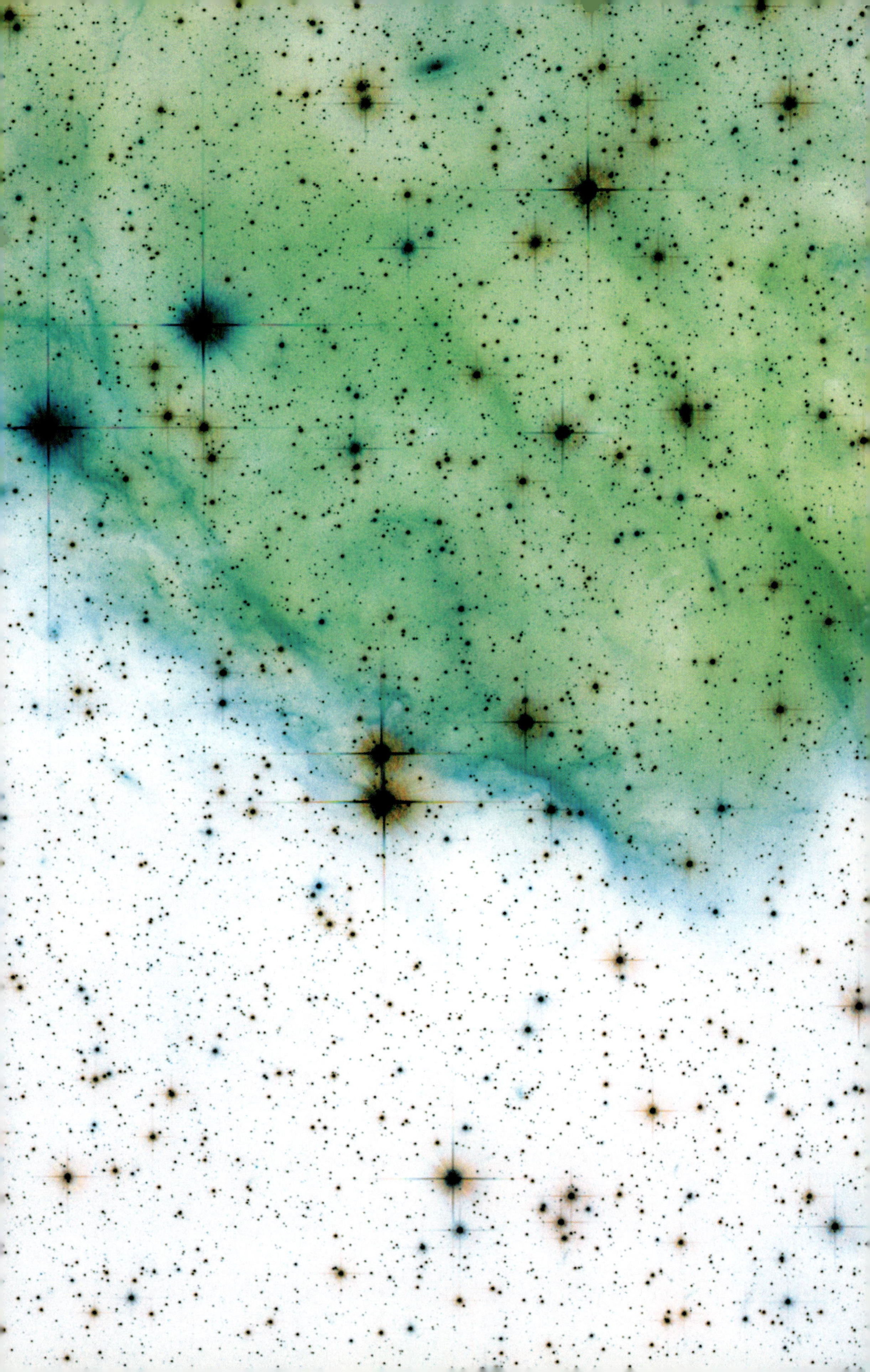

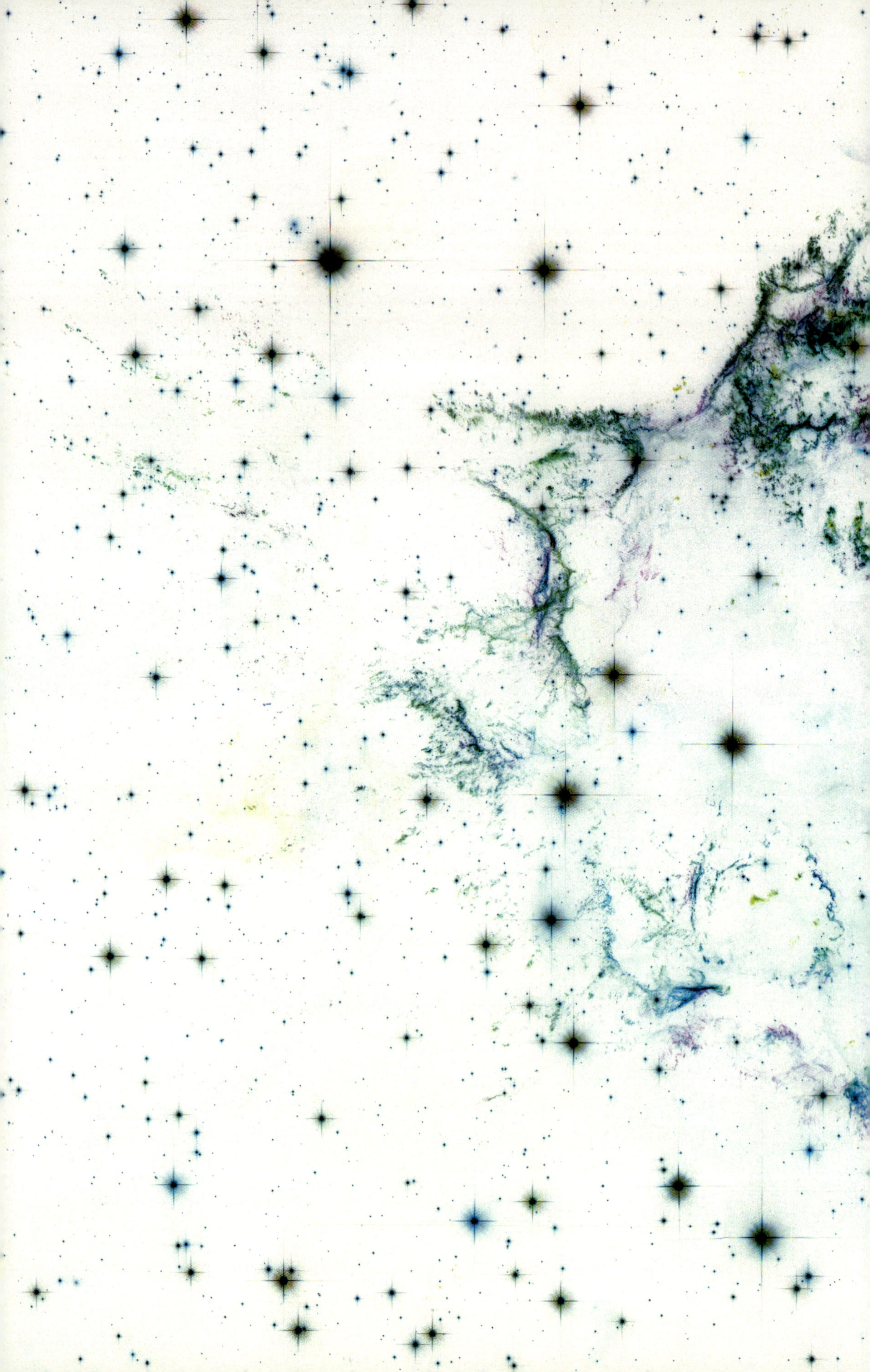

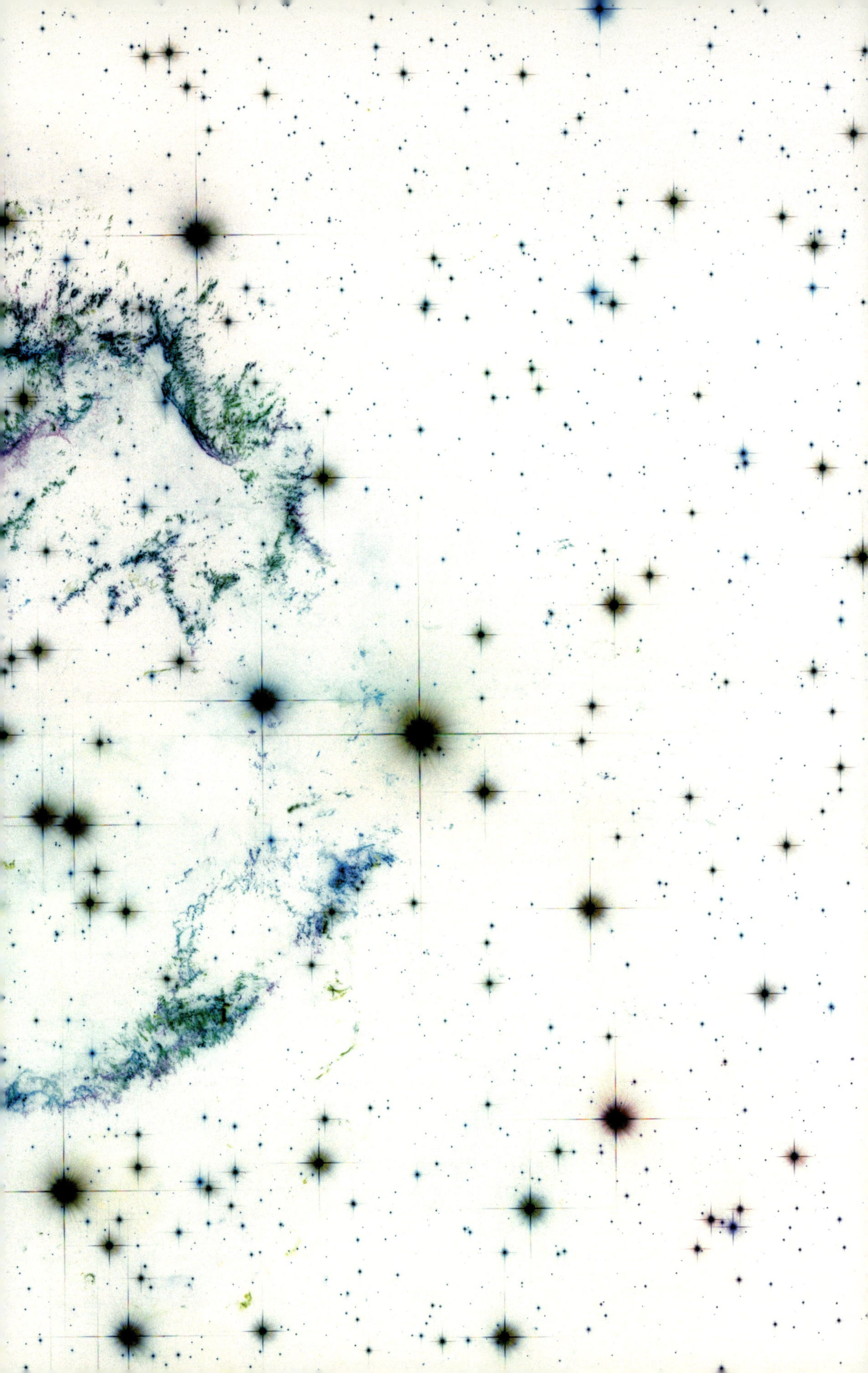

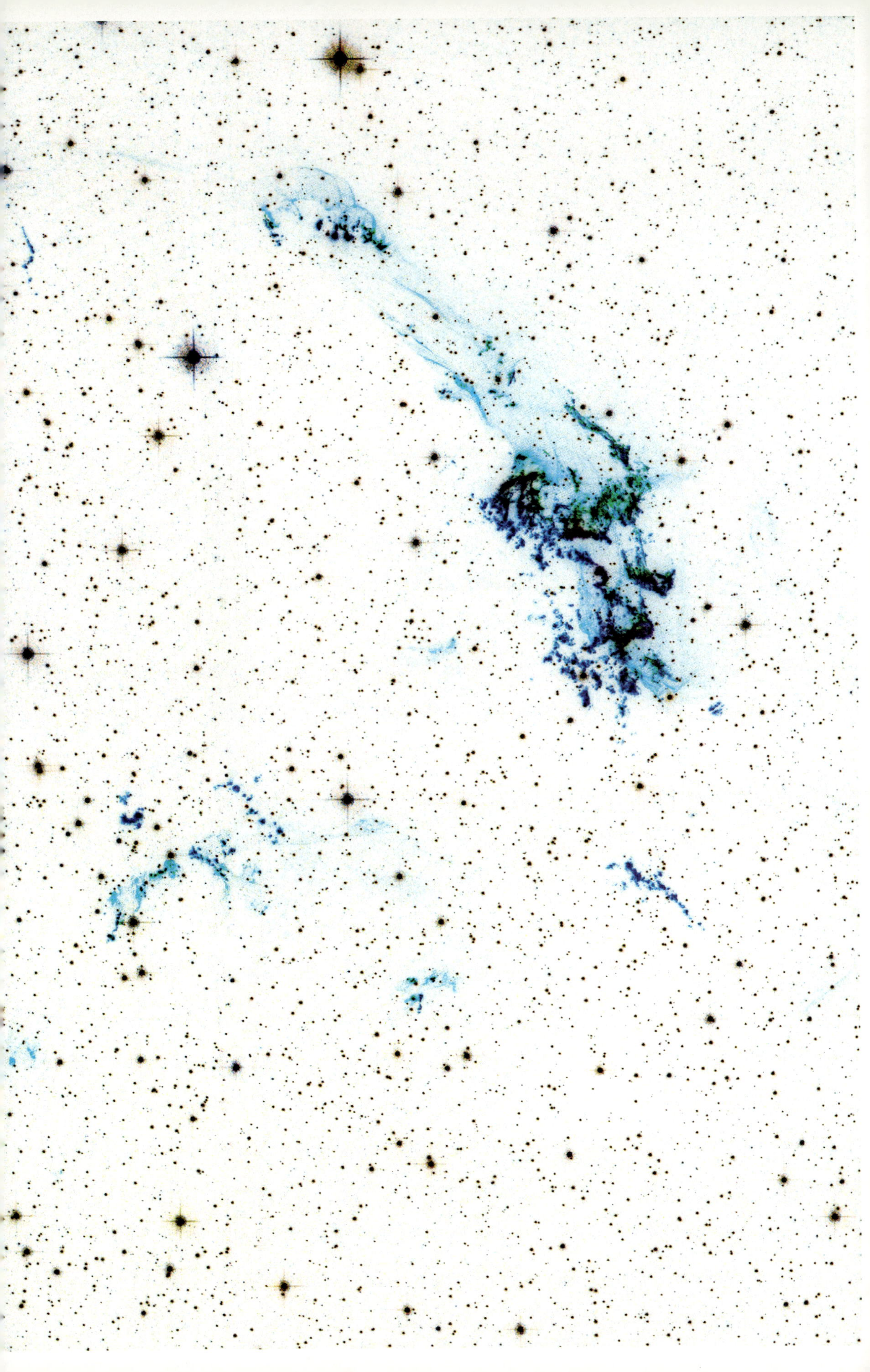

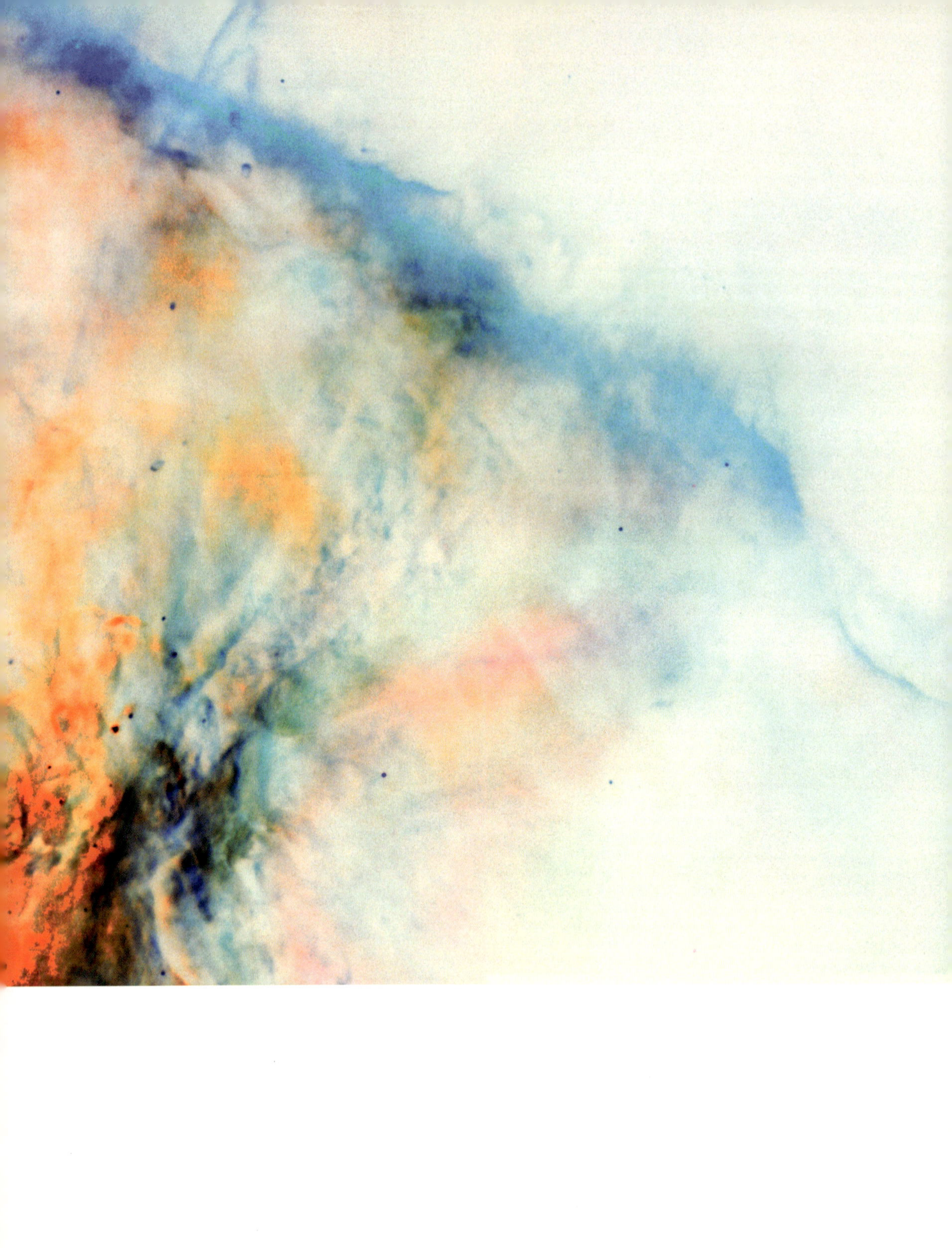

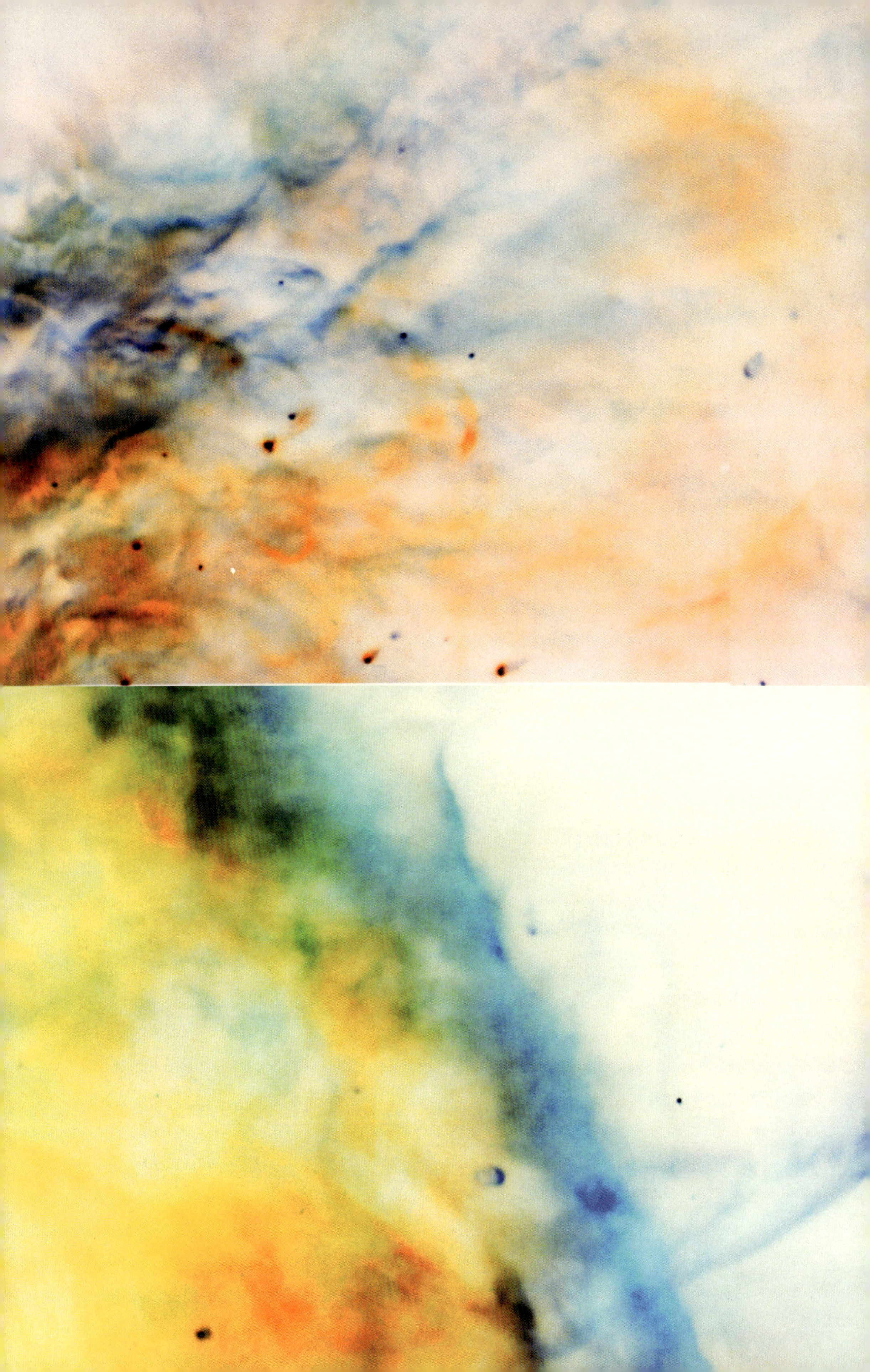

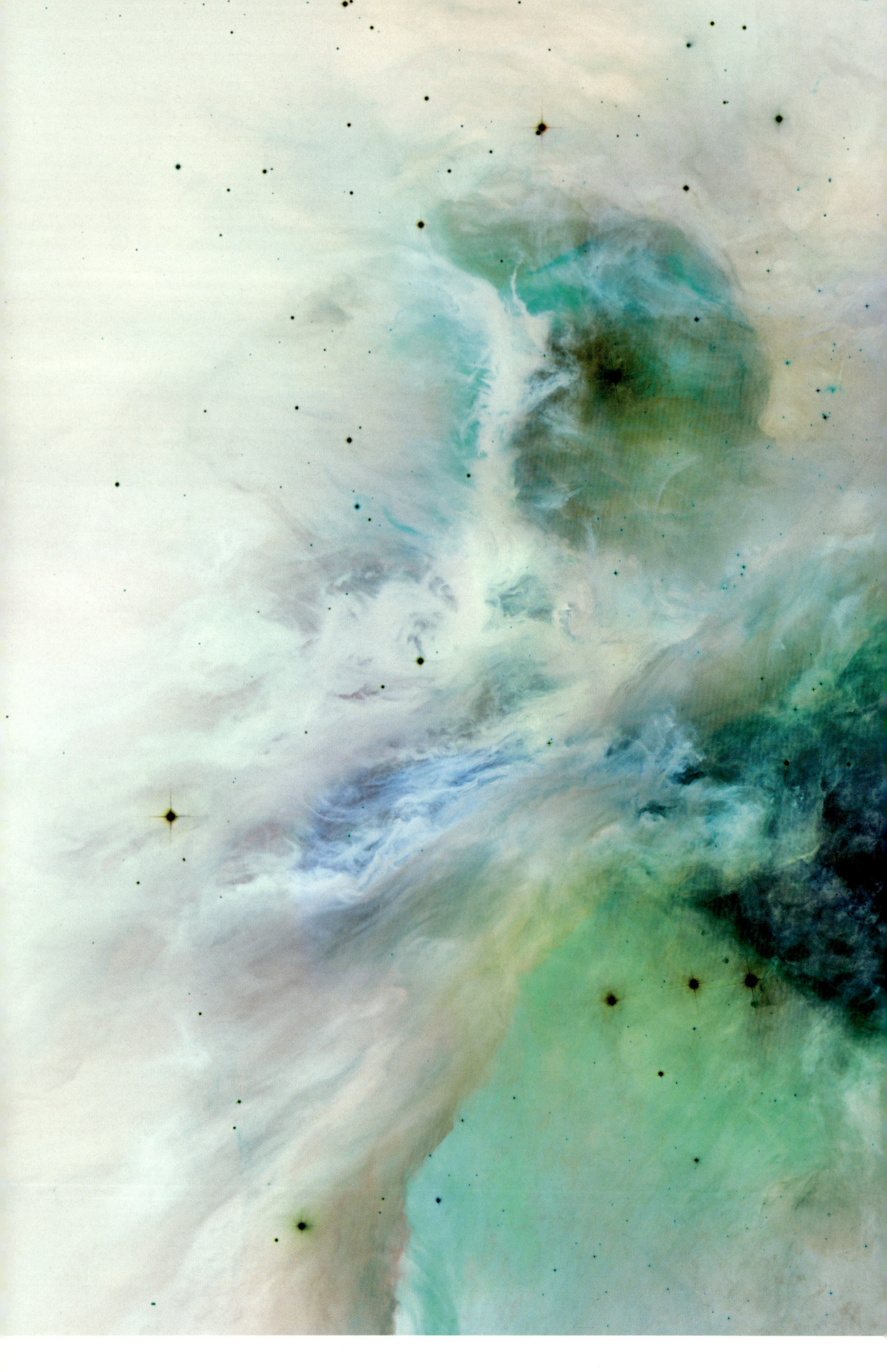

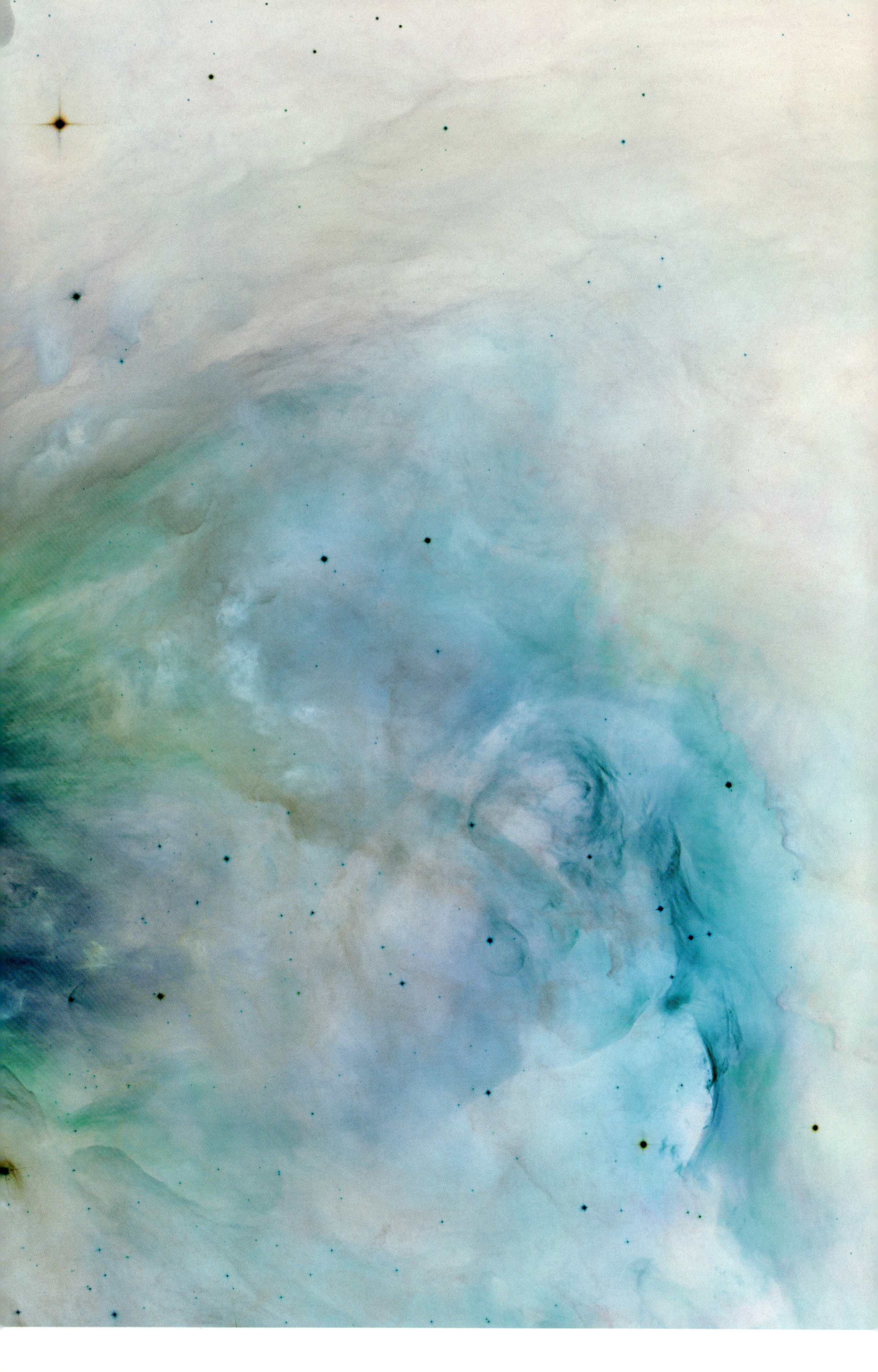

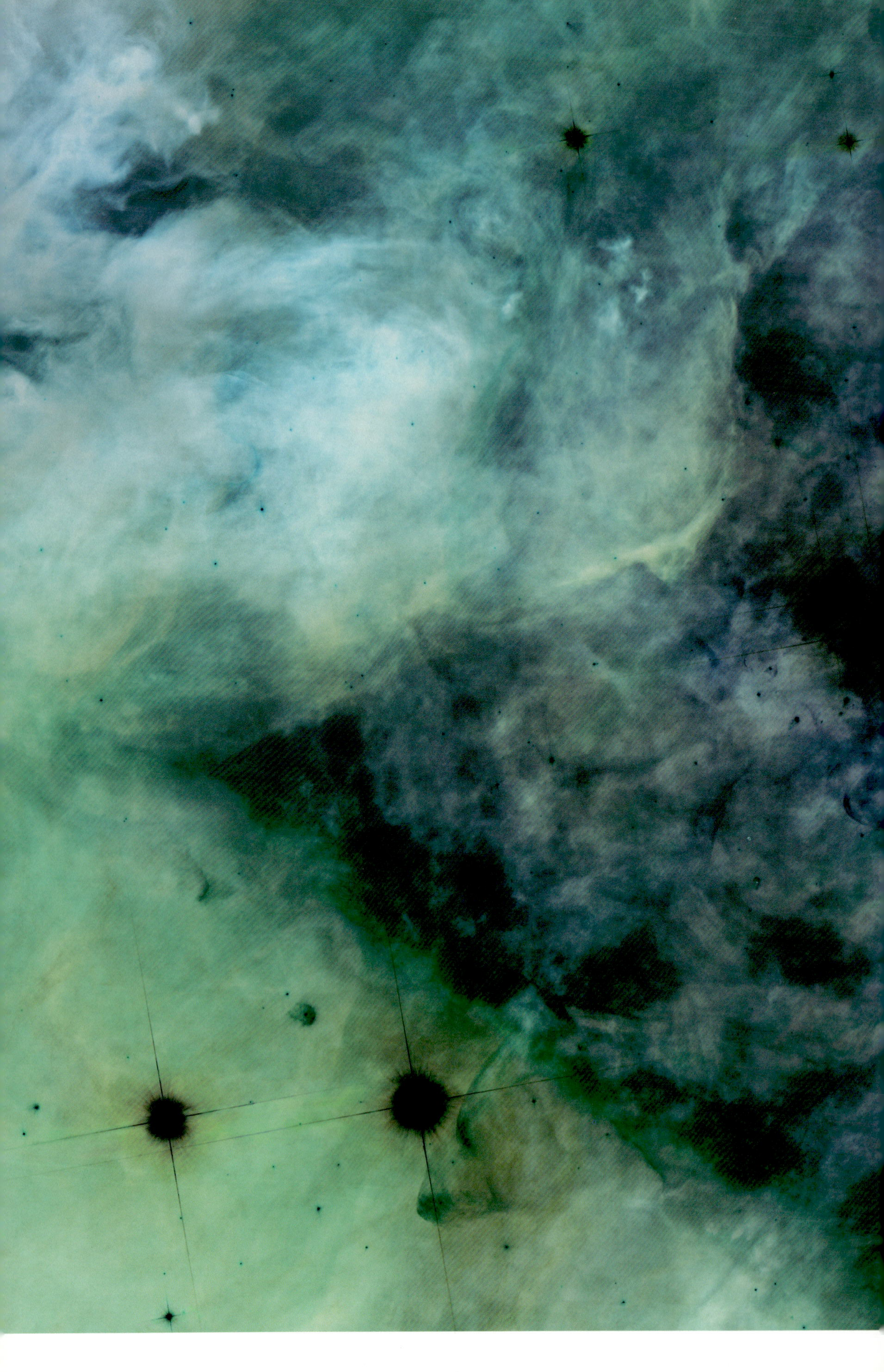

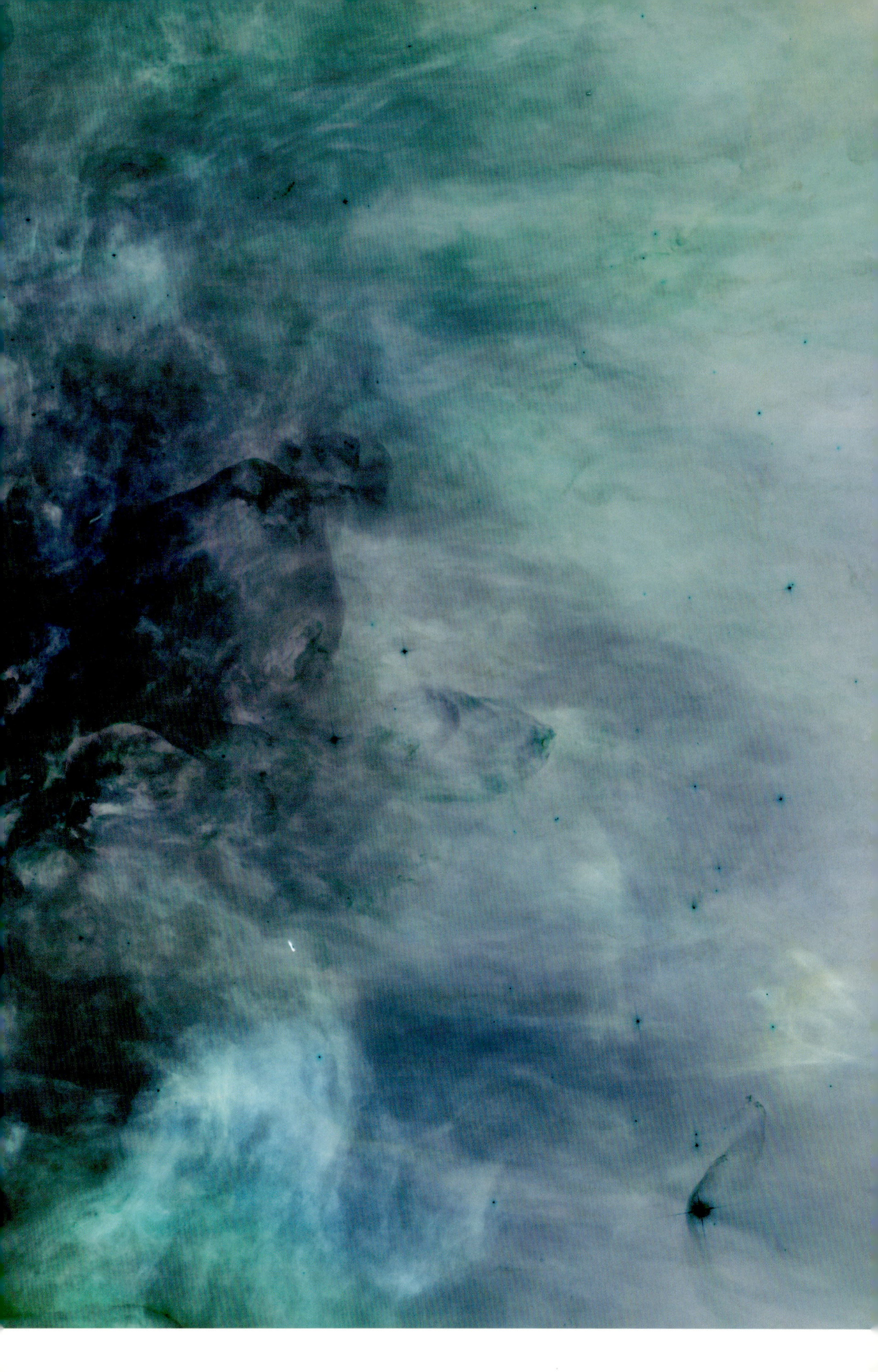

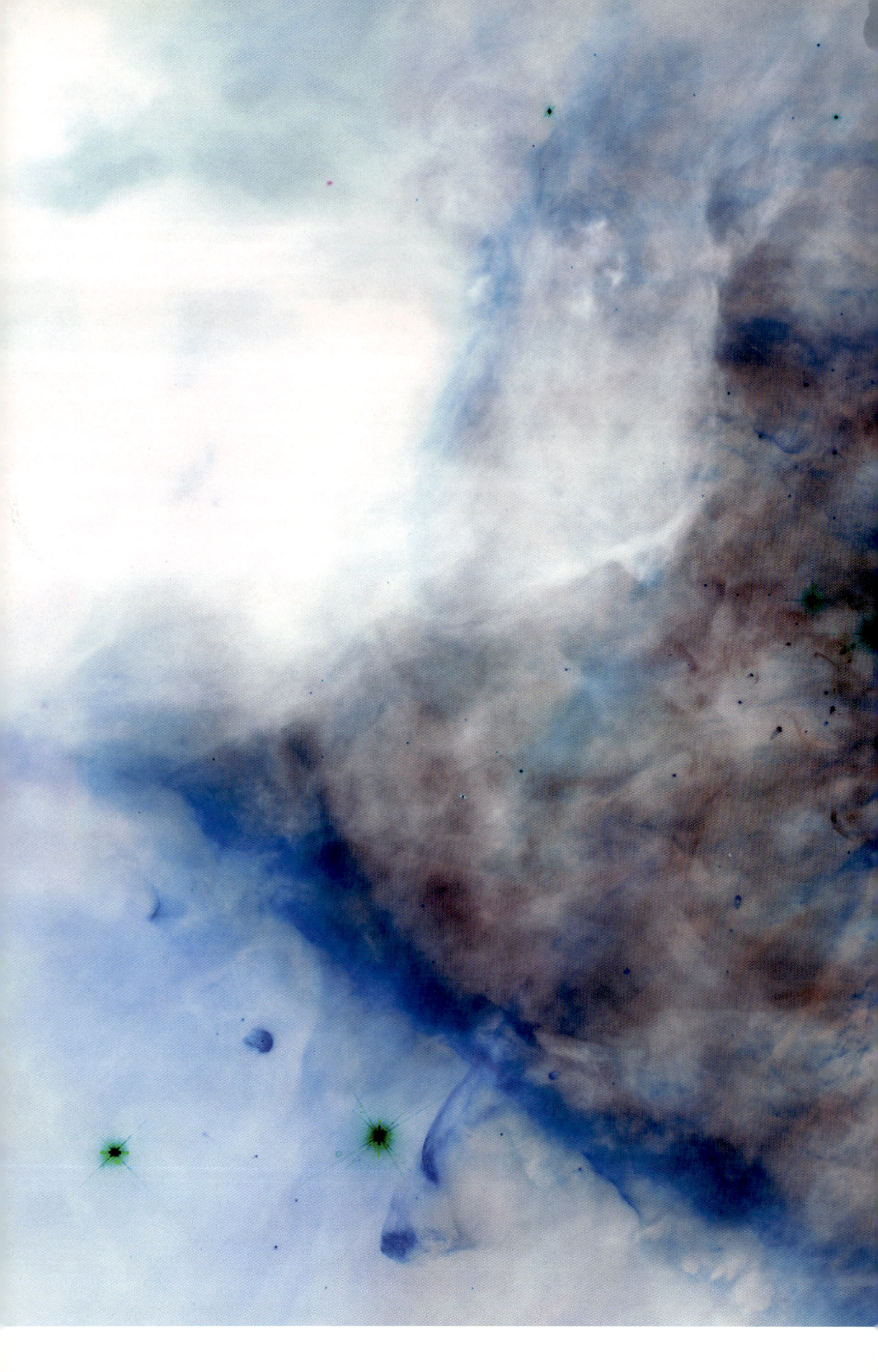

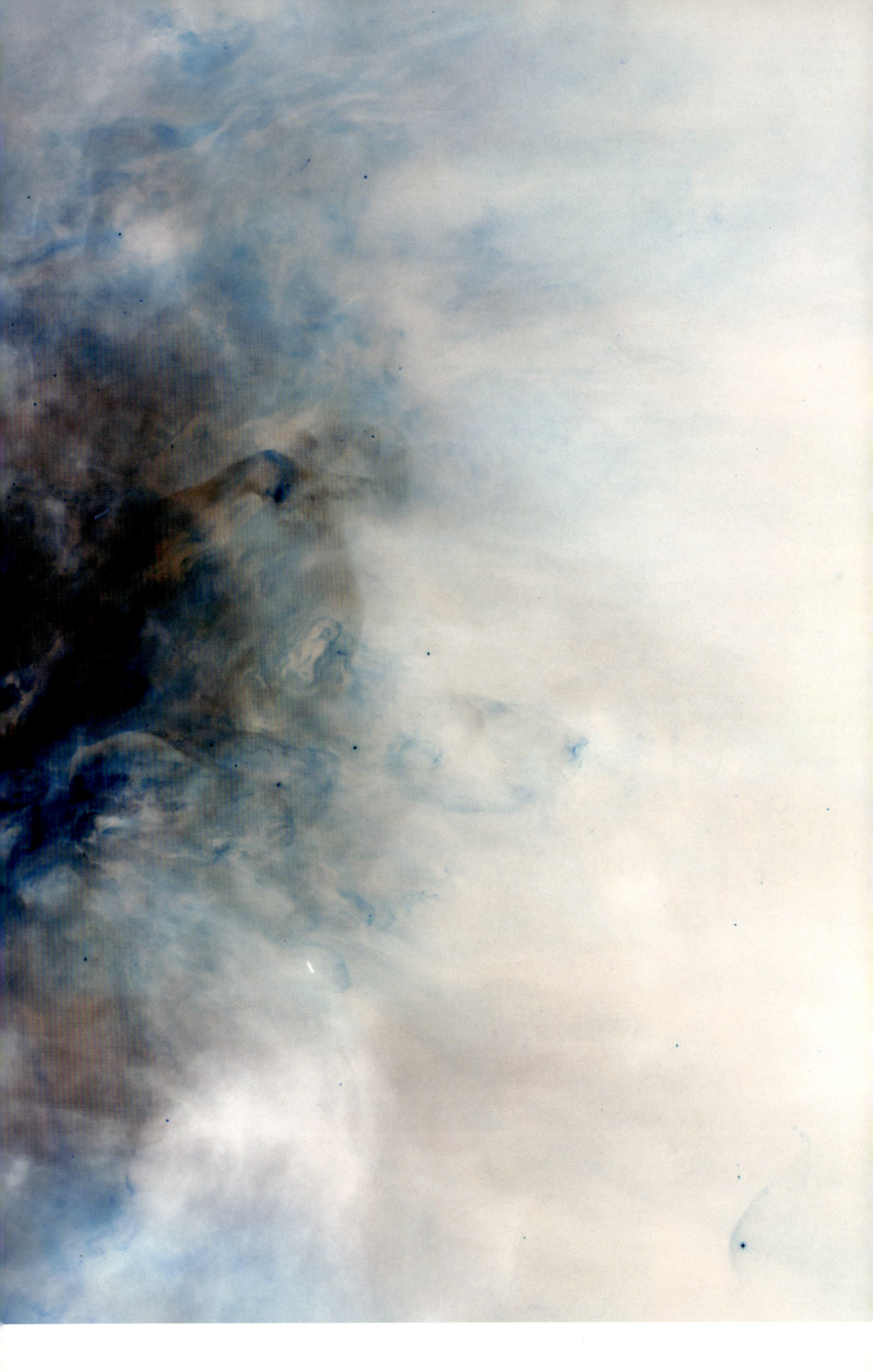

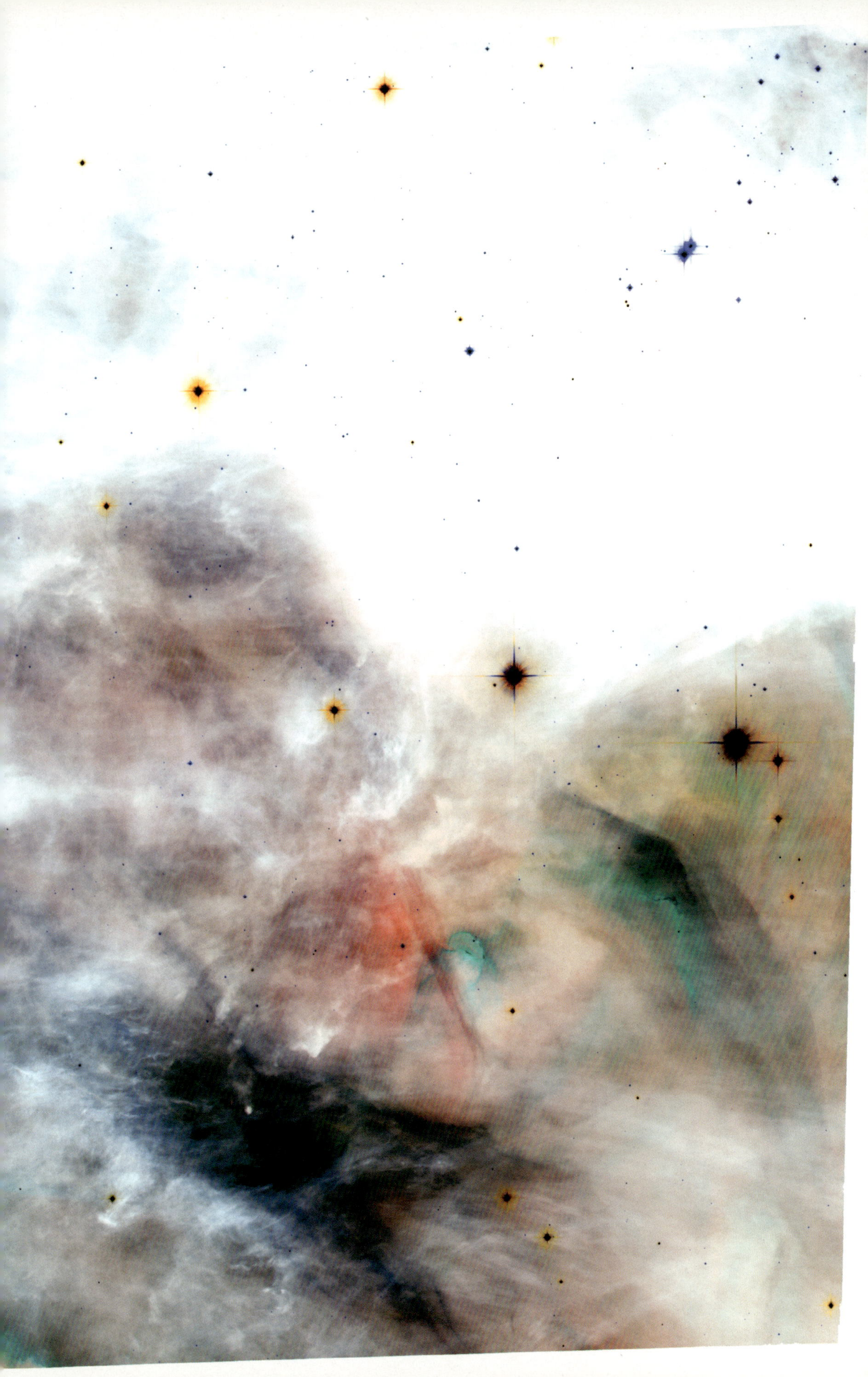

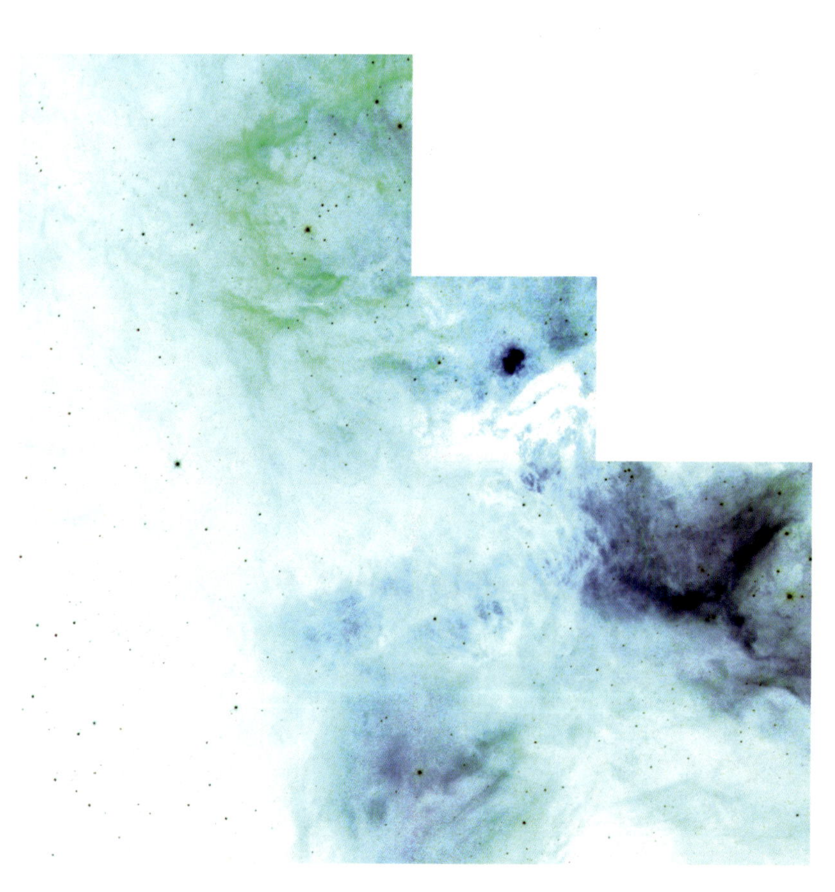

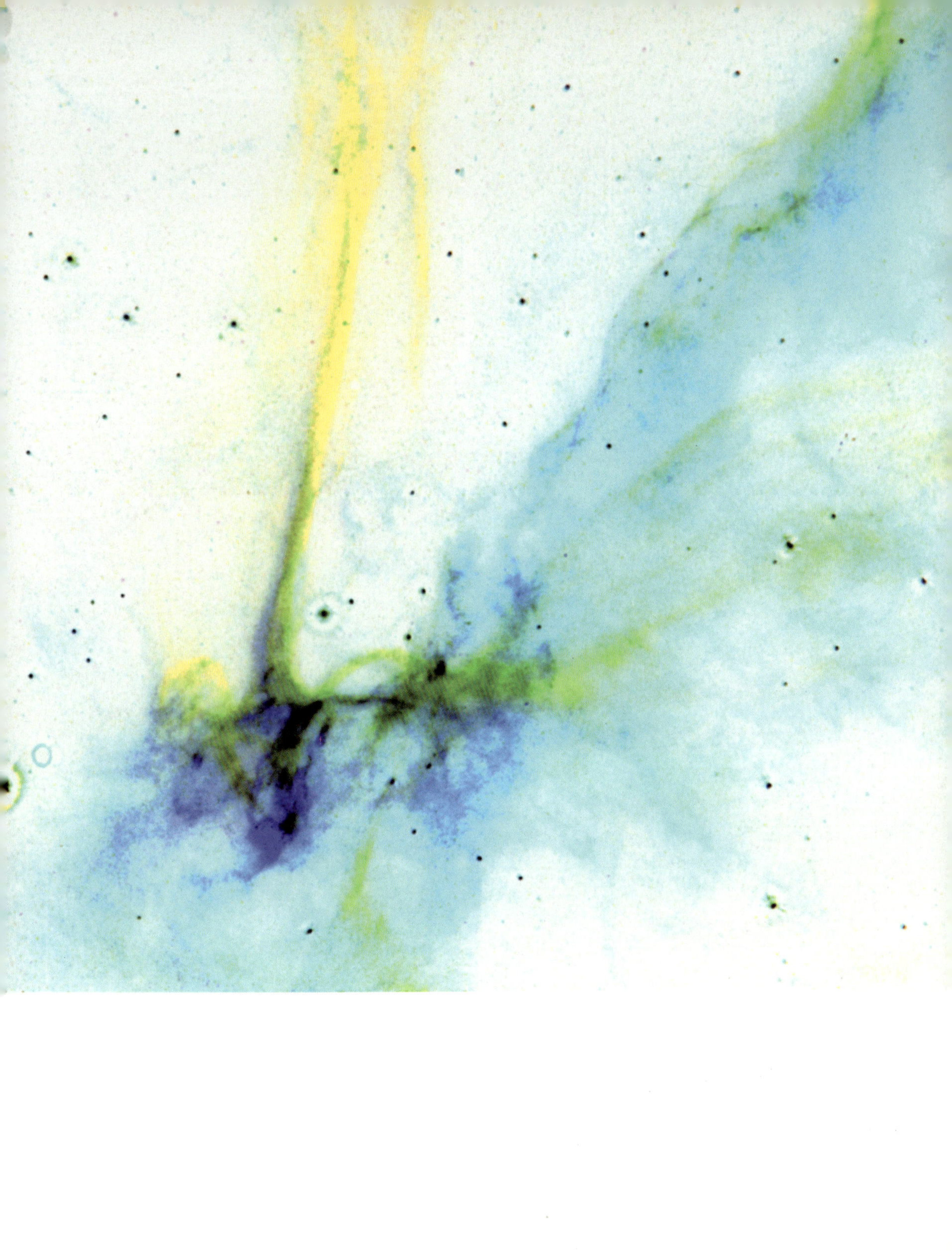

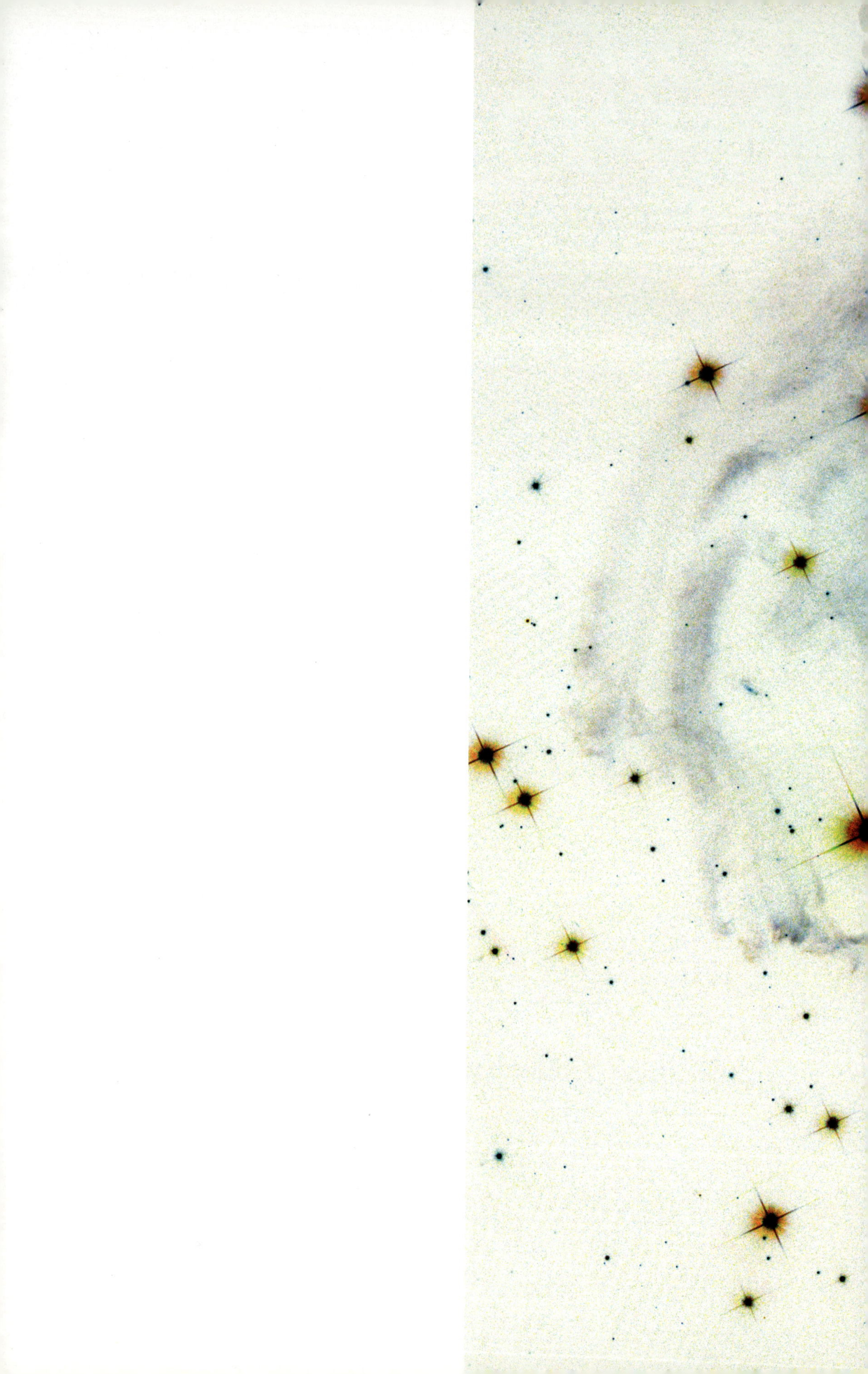

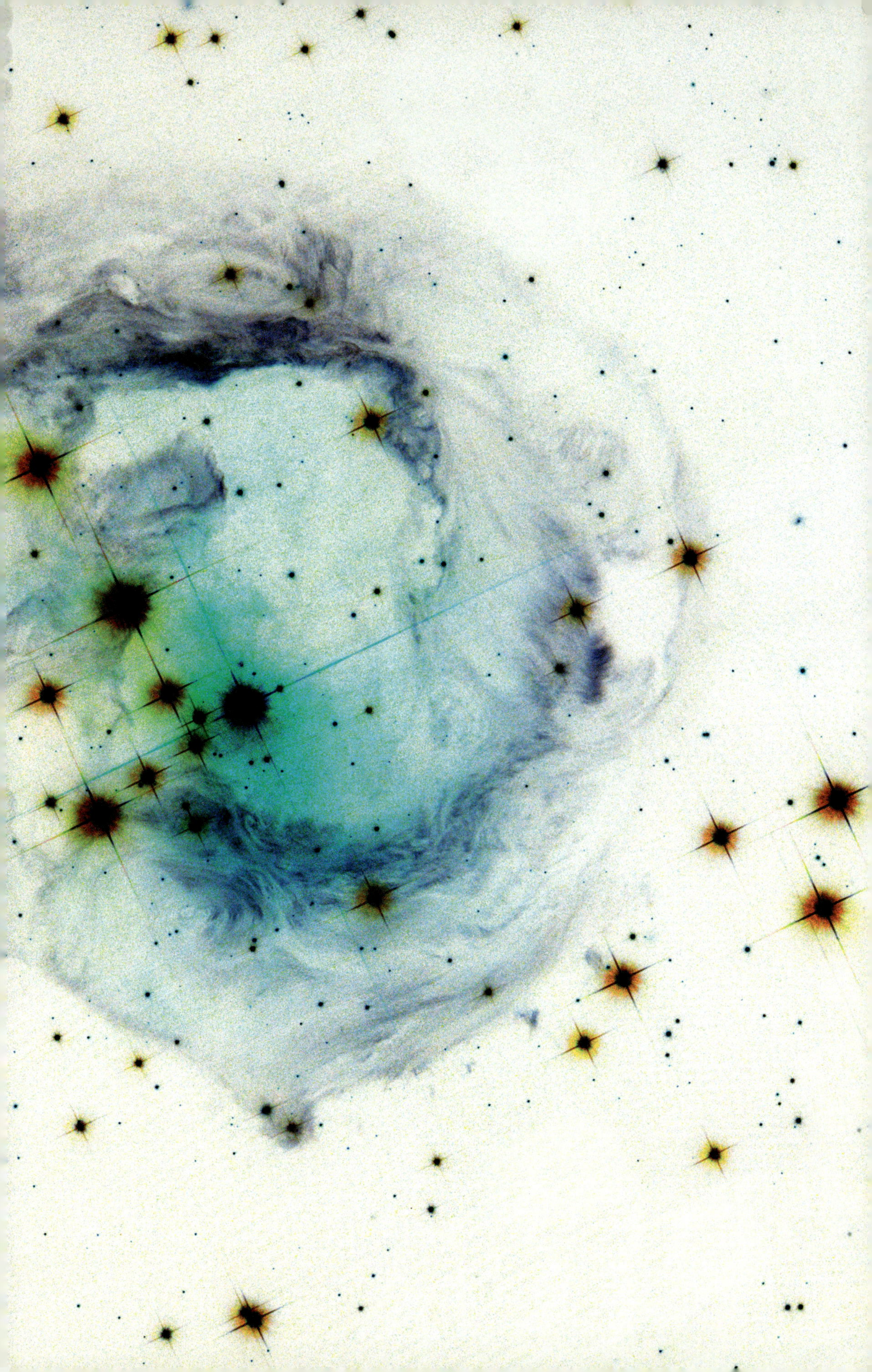

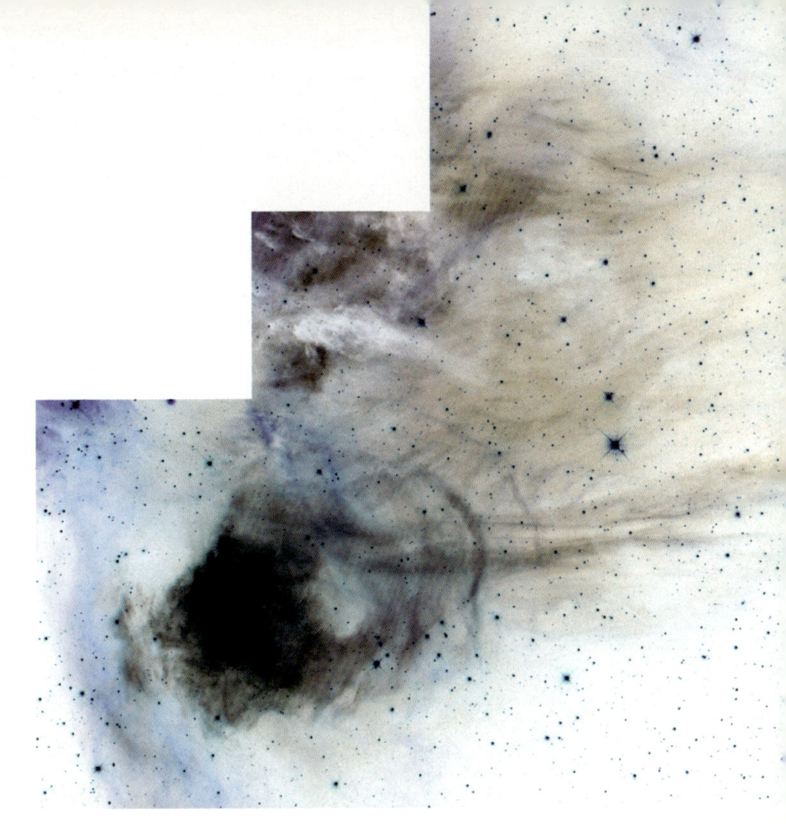

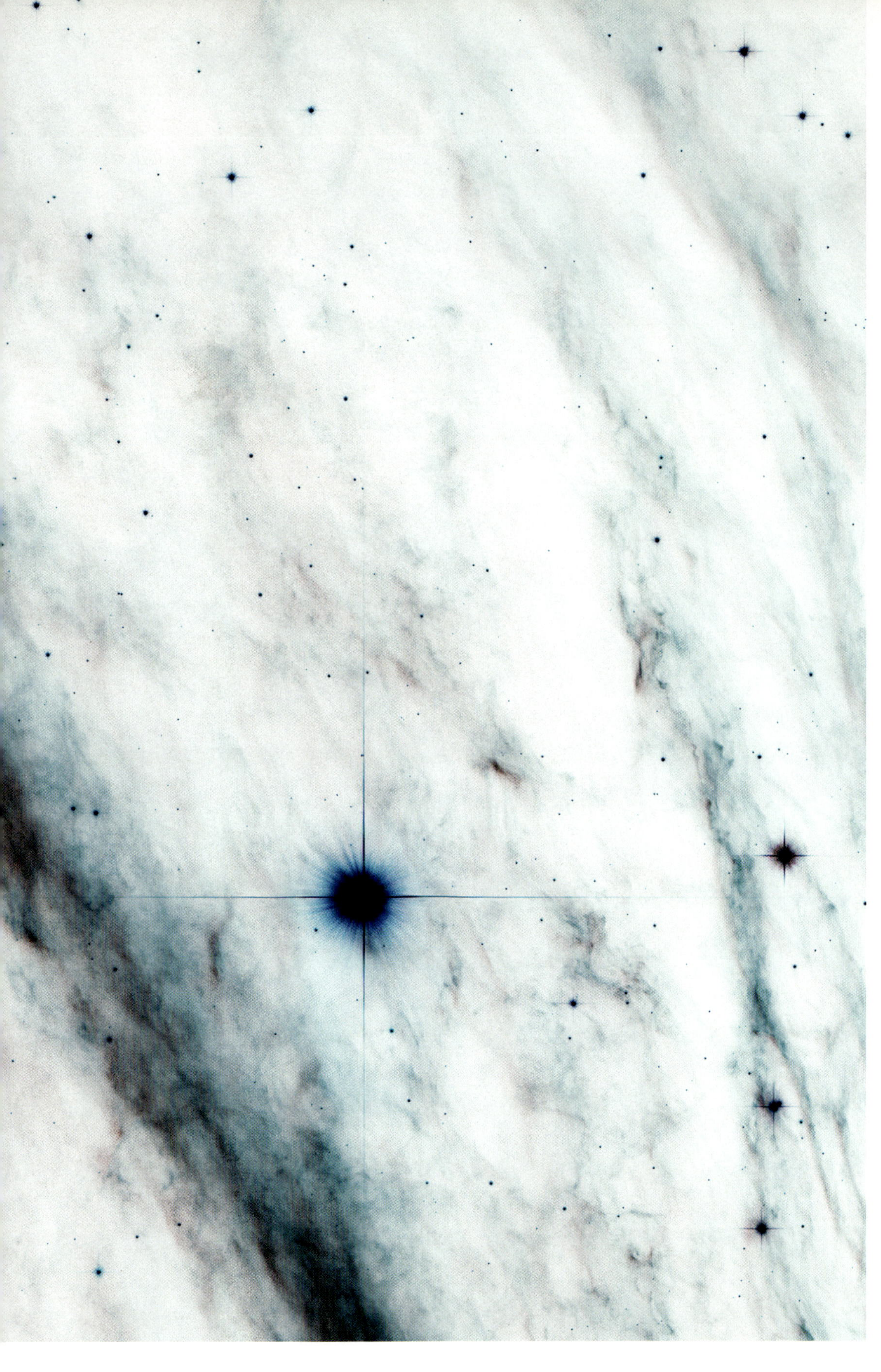

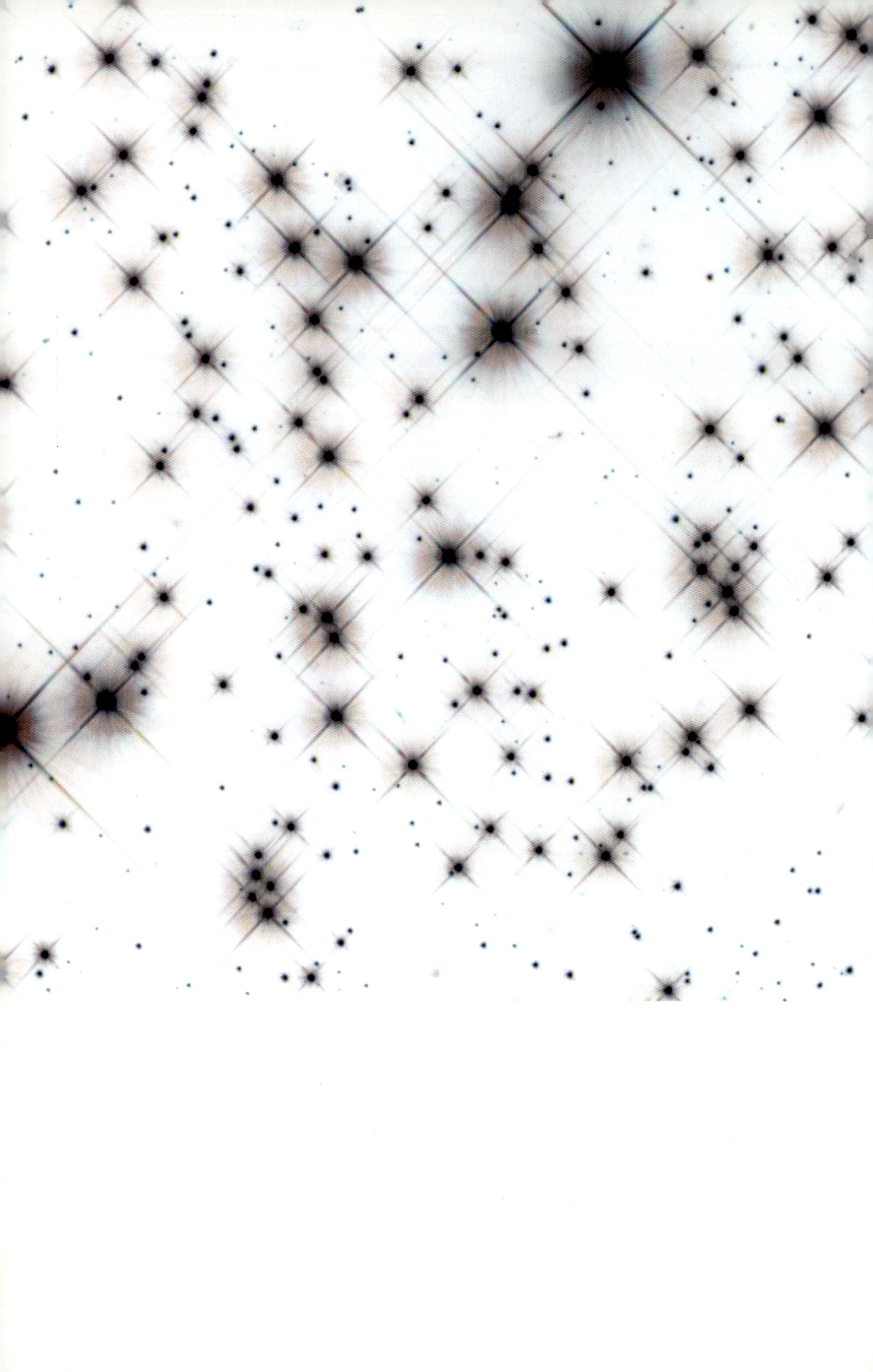

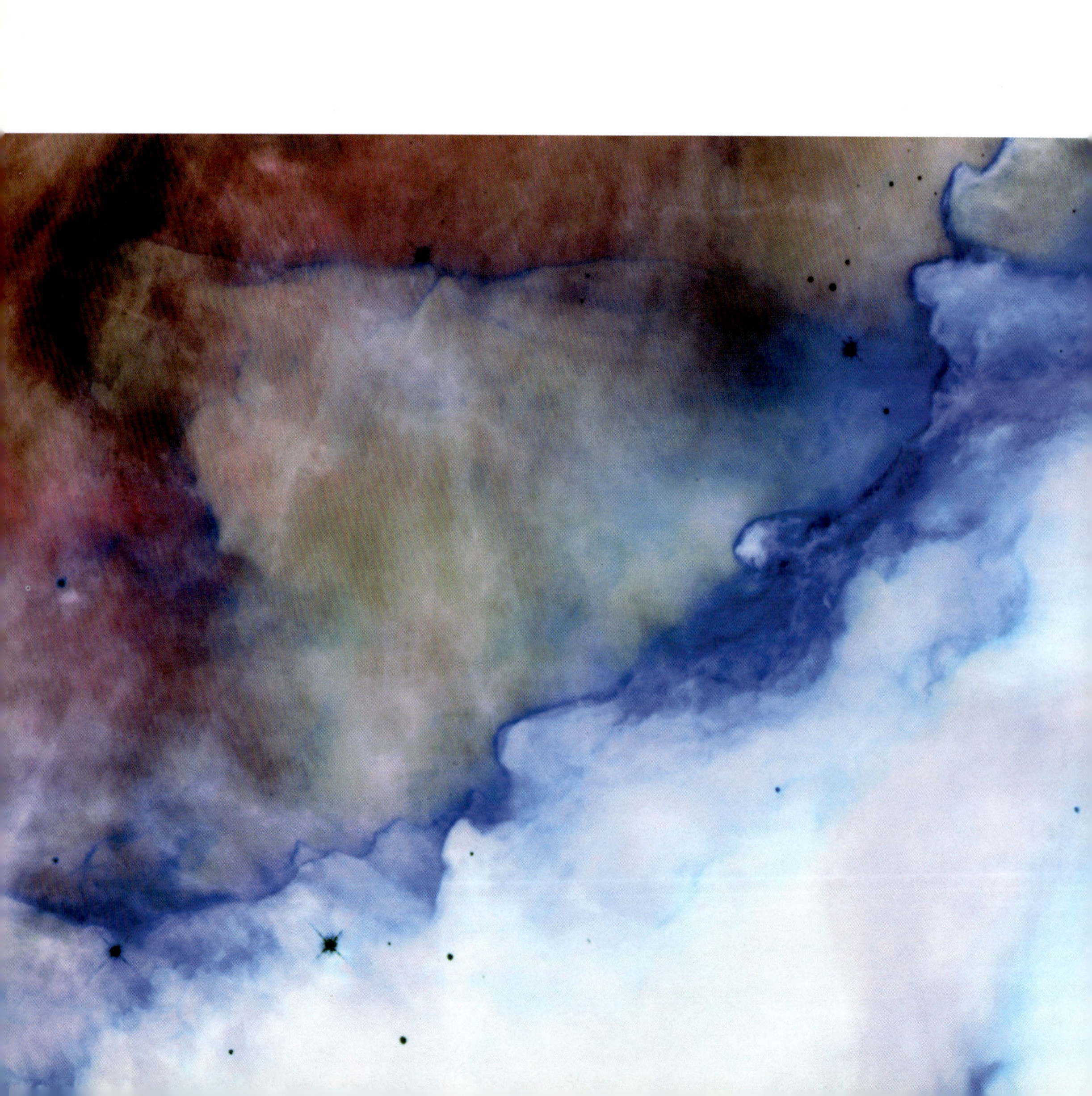

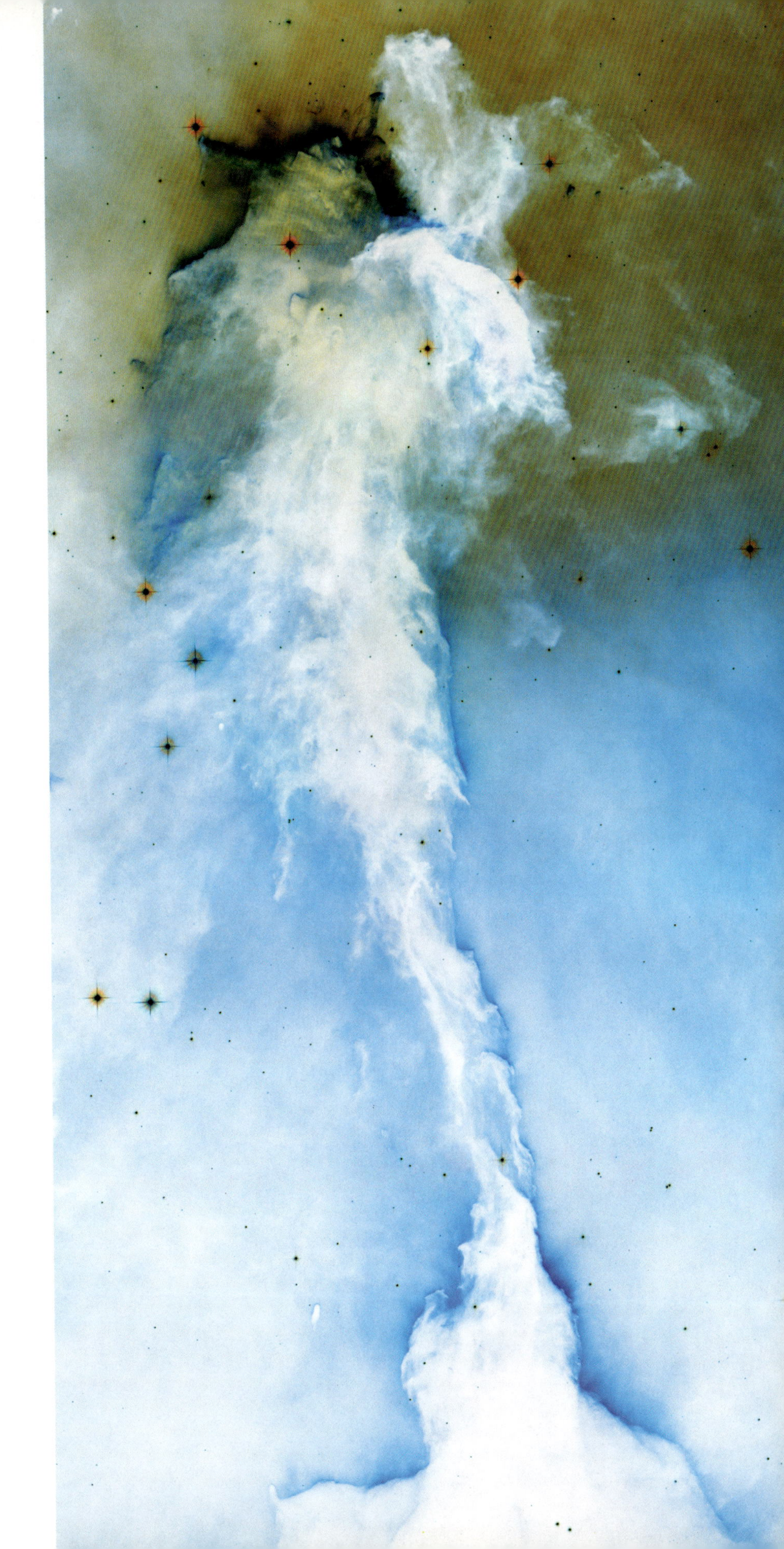

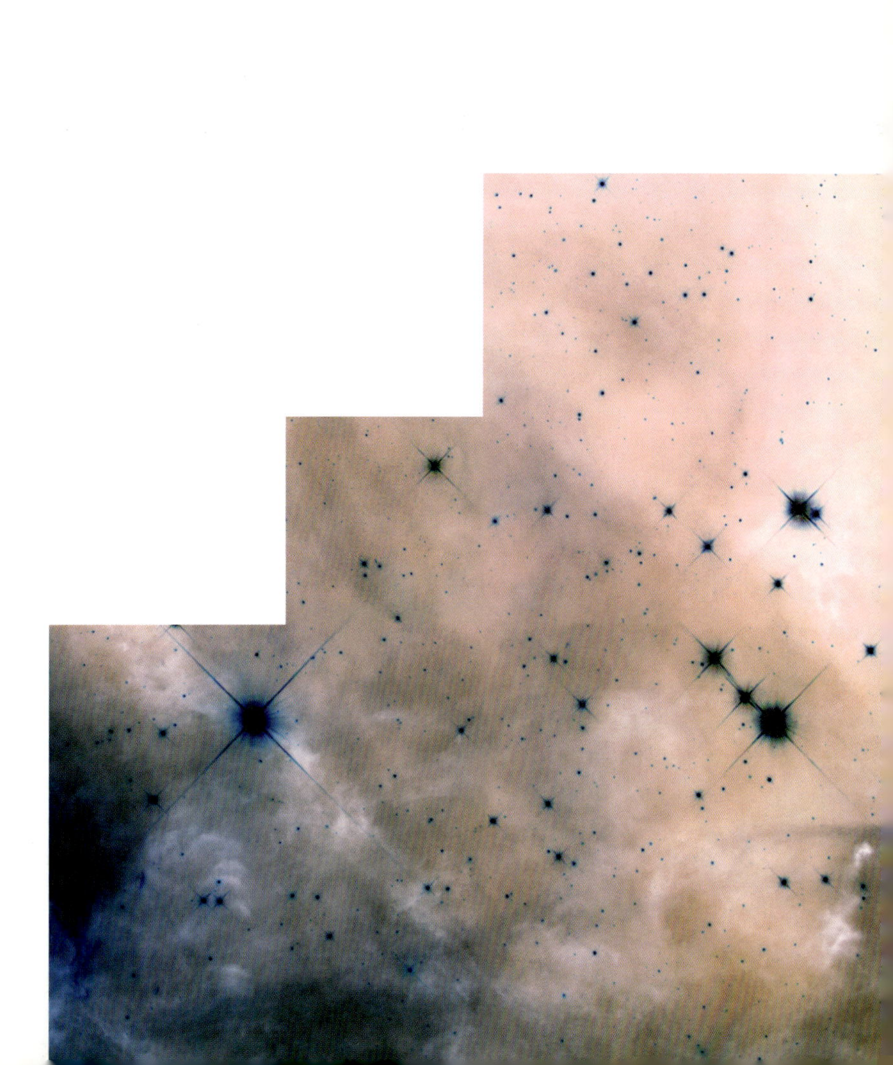

Tutte le immagini in *Negative Space* sono versioni invertite delle fotografie scattate dallo Hubble Space Teleschope.
Le immagini originali sono state prodotte ed elaborate dallo Space Telescope Science Institute (STScI), che ne detiene
la proprietà intellettuale per conto della NASA sotto Contratto NAS 5-26555.

All the images in *Negative Space* are inverted from photographs taken by the Hubble Space Telescope.
The original images were created, authored, and prepared by The Space Telescope Science Institute (STScI)
for NASA under Contract NAS 5-26555.

L'artista ringrazia / The artist thanks Alessandro Rabottini, Christoph Keller, Lionel Bovier, Conny Purtill, Margo Leavin
and Wendy Brandow, John Connelly, Dan Cameron, Zoe Cartledge, Kerry Tribe, The American Academy in Berlin,
NASA and The Space Telescope Science Institute (STScI).

GAMeC - Galleria d'Arte Moderna e Contemporanea
via S. Tomaso, 53
24121 Bergamo - Italy
t +39 035 399529
f +39 035 236962
www.gamec.it

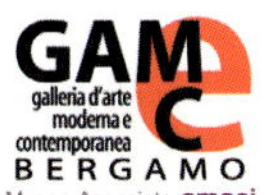

Accademia Carrara

GAMeC - Associazione per la Galleria d'Arte Moderna e Contemporanea di Bergamo   onlus

Soci Fondatori   Soci Benemeriti

 Comune di Bergamo   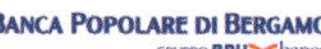 BANCA POPOLARE DI BERGAMO   Si ringrazia per il sostegno
                                              GRUPPO BPU banca   Confindustria Bergamo

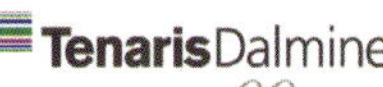 TenarisDalmine   BONALDI

CHRISTOPH KELLER EDITIONS

is a series of artists' books and conceptual art publications, edited, compiled and
selected by Christoph Keller. Published by JRP|Ringier in a limited print run, this specific
edition is aiming to explore the bandwidth of artistic book making and the mediation
of contemporary art in the printed format of the book.

OTHER TITLES IN THIS SERIES:
Helen Mirra, Cloud, the, 3 (ISBN 978-3-905770-17-9)
Jonathan Meese & Slavoj Zizek, Ernteschach dem Dämon (ISBN 978-3-905770-20-9)
Peter Piller, Nijverdal/Hellendoorn (ISBN 978-3-905770-18-6)
Stuart Bailey & Ryan Gander, Appendix Appendix (ISBN 978-3-905770-19-3)
Emmanuelle Antille, Tornados of My Heart (ISBN 978-3-905770-16-2)
Peter Piller, Teilzeitkraft (ISBN 978-3-905770-21-6)

UPCOMING:
Books by Mai-Thu Perret, Michael Stevenson, Johannes Wohnseifer,
Jonathan Monk, Franz Ackermann

PUBLISHED BY:

jrp|ringier

Letzigraben 134
CH-8047 Zurich
T +41 (0) 43 311 27 50
F +41 (0) 43 311 27 51
info@jrp-ringier.com
www.jrp-ringier.com

JRP|Ringier books are available internationally at selected bookstores
and the following distribution partners:

Switzerland: Buch 2000, www.ava.ch
France: Les Presses du réel, www.lespressesdureel.com
Germany and Austria: Vice Versa Vertrieb, www.vice-versa-vertrieb.de
UK: Art Data, www. artdata.co.uk
USA: D.A.P./Distributed Art Publishers, www.artbook.com
Other countries: IDEA Books, www. ideabooks.nl